A Noise in the Garden

A Noise in the Garden

Poems by

Doreen Stock

© 2022 Doreen Stock. All rights reserved.
This material may not be reproduced in any form, published,
reprinted, recorded, performed, broadcast,
rewritten or redistributed without
the explicit permission of Doreen Stock.
All such actions are strictly prohibited by law.

Library of Congress Control Number: 2022931813

ISBN: 978-1-63980-079-7

Kelsay Books
502 South 1040 East, A-119
American Fork, Utah 84003
Kelsaybooks.com

in memory of George Oppen

Acknowledgments

The author would like to thank the editors who first published:

A World Without Wars (The Revolutionary Poets' Brigade, 2019): "To the Gun Dealers"
Birth, (Pure Slush, 2021): "Big Cloud, Little Cloud"
Building Socialism I (Katalumba Press, 2020): "For Susie in Minneapolis"
Building Socialism II (Katalumba Press, 2021): "For Judy in Manhattan"
Bye Bye Blackbird (The Poetry Box, 2021): "Bye Bye Blackbird," "The Butterfly Blouse"
California Quarterly (2020): "Clair de Lune"
Catamaran (2021): "For Aliza, Born in December"
Childhood (The Poet Magazine, 2021): "A Poem of Home Awaits"
Hope (TL;DR Press, 2021): "The Fishpond and Rabbi Ilfi"
Kayak (1973): "Poem of the Three Incarnations"
MPC Anthology (2020): "In Transit, The Galapagos," "I Dream of Snow"
Pandemic Puzzle Poems (Blue Light Press, 2021): "On the Death of John Prine"
Puerto Del Sol (1976): "Of the Great Cats"
Stories & Poems to the Song of Life Anthology, (Sweetycat Press, 2022) "Lenski'sAria on the Lips of my Granddaughter"
Tango Man (Finishing Line Press, 2020): "The Cigar of Fidel"
Trampoline: A Poetry Journal (2021) *Issue 5:* "A Noise in the Garden"

Cover Art: "Path," an etching by Susan B. Weissman, framed by elements of a digital painting, "Orange Feathers" by Sophia Drozd. Author Photo: "At the Museum of Science," by Amy Stock Drozd.

I would like to thank Judy Brackett Crowe and Debbi Handler for their help in shaping this manuscript, Stephen Kessler for his generous appraisal of it, as well as Jack Hirschman, Barbara Swift Brauer, Jackie Kudler, and Kathy Evans for their continual support of my work. Gratitude too, to the entire editorial and design staff at Kelsay Books.

Contents

I. A Noise in the Garden—2015

A Noise in the Garden	14
Poem of the Three Incarnations	19
Of the Great Cats	24
Man, Head in Hand, Resting on the Banks of the Euphrates	26
Mathematics of the Violated	27
Parisians Moving into Light, November 2015	28
Tango of the Sleeping Giant	29
A Poem of Home Waits	31
Footfalls, March 2015	32
On Leaving the Academy of Science	33

II. The Butterfly Blouse—2016

The Butterfly Blouse	36
Two from Lufthansa	38
Your Art in Times of Sadness	40
Waving	41
The Great Bliss Queen Meets Omar	42
The Compliment	43
Seven Bathers in the Garden of Victoria Ocampo	44
On Not Being Recognized	45
Man in Bed with Me	46
I Saw the President Dance	47

III. The Tree of Wheat—2017

Rabbi Yehuda and the Tree of Wheat	50
Binyamin the Shepherd and I	52
Why Rav Adda bar Ahava Stood on the Banks of the Dannak River	54

Big Cloud, Little Cloud	55
From a Letter to Rilke	56
Como Tu	57
For Sharon Doubiago on the 5th of July	58
Peanut-Butter-and-Jellies	60
Simple Math	61

IV. Paper Dolls—2018

Paper Dolls	64
From a Letter to Rilke, #2	66
On Eating Walleye Pike at the St. Paul Grill	67
One Sunday Afternoon	68
Poem on the Earth Moving South	70
Rabbi Tweeting the Un-Tweetable	74
Prayer to Be Said on Entering an American Synagogue	75
The Cigar of Fidel	76
Clair de Lune	79
Poem in Which I Dream I Am the Newly Elected President of Mexico	80
For Prosper in Jerusalem	81

V. If a Star Could Talk—2019

If a Star Could Talk	84
For Aliza, Born in December	86
"Lenski's Aria" on the Lips of My Granddaughter	87
Bye Bye Blackbird	88
On Metaphor	89
To the Gun Dealers	90
As Vinegar to the Teeth as Smoke to the Eyes	91

A Marten, Two Girls, a Pit	92
The Fishpond and Rabbi Ilfi	94
In Transit, The Galapagos	95

VI. I Dream of Snow—2020

The Well	98
On the Death of John Prine	100
For Judy in Manhattan	101
For Susie in Minneapolis	102
On Seeing the Comet Noewise	103
Man Dreaming	104
I Dream of Snow	105
About the Author	106

I. A Noise in the Garden—2015

A Noise in the Garden

> According to legend, King David tried to postpone the hour of his death by reading God's law without stopping, knowing that the Angel of Death could not take his soul while he was studying. The Angel got tired of waiting and entered the garden behind the royal palace, where he made a loud noise. Hearing it, David left his studies and descended into the garden by way of some steps to see what it was. One of the steps gave way. The King fell down and was killed instantly...
> —a *midrash*

Each turn of the head
is made
into destiny

into the black bush
carved silent on the glass

We move and move
it is a slow breathless
dance, it is dark

and braced with flame
at every edge

the stone the fruit the tree
globed and iridescent

our tongues are the bells
our flesh sweats and screams

When the King turned
to watch us

his hour flew from him
in heavy bands and awful

wings…
                        *

At the open gate
a dead thrush
the children touching
its neck

the dirt sifting
over its body
over the little hairs
surrounding its eye

buried by my children
until all I could see
was the dot of pain
that once was its vision

its song was covered
its curled feet covered

and night came over
the small space
and rained down its stars

and sun came over
the small space
and filled it
with the disappearance of meat
and the disappearance of effort

(such effort as a bird makes
to gather its life)

and certain words of the children
certain of the orange feathers
sent themselves down
to flame in all the nearby lilies.

*

What happens to people when they are dead?
you asked on the exact day of your birth at two
in the afternoon. Four years old today and the light
spilling down the redwood trunks outside our window
me in the dining room chair where I then sat to face
you in your question your eyes so clear and large
black trees glowing in them

just this morning in the dream
I pulled a blue knit cap
over your bright hair like
when you were only two

(and once before
we were separated
and I called and called
you but you answered to
a new name
I awoke then thinking of the
King)

"Maybe they build houses
under the ground," you said

Maybe.

"I think they grow feathers there, too."

Do you think so?

"Yes."

Oh, Ben, the gates of all our days
are red and gold. Once upon a time,
a winter night, a fast furious
brilliant pain inscribed a moment
so fine I live toward and away from
it always. You and I
through every darkness.
How we come to exist.

Remember.
We shatter the night.
We are the green.

Poem of the Three Incarnations

The Salmon

You pull them effortlessly from the sea
their blood and silver skins heavy with
crowns

You land them one after another
at my feet

We laugh and eat the sweet orange meat
the white wine falls into our cupped hands

Oh look, it's spilling into our whole boat
you are turning and laughing
we are turning and laughing

Our bellies are up and blue
we slip over the edge to lie
in the dark for years and years

Then somewhere the single book we made
with our sides is flayed open

There are no words in it
only our precise bones

The hand of a child touches them

Unthinking thrusts them into the mouth

When one of our bones
sticks in the child's throat

That cry means
we are just now understood.

The Bees

They come hidden in the red leaves
They come as the want to just touch
something sharp
And the leaves were stiff and there were
after all so many of them
the smell of smoke and wet dust

I don't remember kneeling
only the armfuls and armfuls
of edges and a pricking of my cheeks
and flinging and digging and making
huge circles as if they were snow

And the wings in my ear throbbing like
too much blood in my neck all at once
or letters being opened
or the thick silk sleeves I make for you

And my two hands always open to receive
this darkness running straight up my arms
to where the breath begins and ends

Bees, bees, the honey black with red blades
the body soft pulsing drinking wine-colored
water stinging even in the eyelids and the soles
of my feet until I am wide with their language

Bees.

The Deer

In the margin of what once was our life
someone laughed in a single bell and said:

You are given to awaken in each other's
arms just one time
you may choose the place

There was no hesitation
We reached out one hand and touched
the spot between the eyes of the gray
deer as it stood silent in the garden

Her forehead opened and we were given
the light all the way back of the cave
We were given her blood we were given
her mouth

You became the left half of her jaw
and I became the right half
where we came together we were given
rain wind moon sun

We felt it all be real in our bodies
it hurt and was exquisite all at once

Then when we had to leave each other
in our separate mouths we began to taste
earth

We ran our tongues over it
We knew nothing of language then or time
but as we laughed and wept the taste
kept growing like mountains
and finally we said:
This is morning.

Of the Great Cats

who lie side by side of the warm wind
each hair against the sand

whose bodies are surrounded in an air gigantic
with flesh smoke-scented ringing red circles
that move behind our eyes

who lick each other until they are tight with our vision
who ransom the entire desert floor with juices that course
to the mouth

whose eyes are stones on each other

who shift and heave who float above cities
who cause all the nations to march through them
with nails who pull the elements of destruction
through their throats who are atomic
whose bones are etched with arrows and crowns
who draw from their entrails
words to be written on the blade:

"The lightning of a Lance for the Power of God"
"Shootings of Blood to make the Slain Fall
in the Anger of God"
"Flashing of a Sword Consuming the Iniquitous
Slain in the Judgment of God"

who spit god, god who turn on the white core
who make it a fire who hold the doll in their teeth
who worry the red bird who are lighting it all

whose sex is soft and retracted
in the darkness
who roll on the black core
who are wet and always separate

who bring the full moon down
to sit on their shoulders
like a scorched egg

and leap
to shake it free

Man, Head in Hand, Resting on the Banks of the Euphrates

A *militiaman*, a *Kurd*, a *terrorist*, or an *anti-Islamic*, he sits in worn pants and high-top tennis shoes on a barricade, camouflage jacket zipped closed against the cold, the heat, or just to keep his heart in his chest cavity...

On his left wrist he's wearing a watch with a minute hand, a second hand, or perhaps two dots separating his hours from his minutes, sandbags, empty metal drums, rubbled rock surrounding a blood pressure, some arteries and veins, the customary skeletal bones...

Slumped in exhaustion, defeat, despair, prayer, we cannot tell, his eyes closed against his palm. And what image floats upon the screen his soul pulls down for him in this instant of calm before the next bomb goes off and living or dead he hits the dust at his feet...

from a *New York Times* photograph by Tyler Hicks

Mathematics of the Violated

As we were flying we saw them coming again
spraying us with their boiling yellow gasses.
As we were flying we tried to avoid the brown and yellow
and I reached back to grasp the hand of my father
who was also flying.

We were weeping the same tears that taught us in the
beginning how to fly. "I have a mathematical plan,"
said our father, "and it's about division."

So we divided. At first it was so hard, I, I have never been a
tree branch or a leaf on that branch, or a path of earth, or a
stone on that path. But we did it, what he said, dividing
ourselves into the newly inhabited trees and leaves, into paths,
into stones, and in the end he was correct, our father,
because this kind of flying, leaving our bodies behind
ourselves under Them, is not a thing to be wished on anyone.

Parisians Moving into Light, November 2015

How seamlessly the light takes over as they are ripped from wine, music, conversation in this gang war grown up into the wrong side of God, and killed for seeking pleasure as green seeks yellow and yellow seeks white

So red they are pink, so yellow, white, clouds sweep their new crowns with blisters of light, so red they are pink, so yellow, white leaves falling, letters rising, the lone soldier marching in the dark, guarding the lit schoolroom window

left to right.

Tango of the Sleeping Giant

1

Step by step
you execute the medical techno-tango
black jacket against the sudden drop
in temperature

step by step down the blue hall
of an Argentine cancer clinic

moving stealthily
in the giant's castle.

We can hear him snoring.
We can pray that he doesn't wake
Not till you have done with this
Particular *milonga, Tanguero.*

Step, breathe
Step, breathe

If he wakes
he could make us a whole lot of trouble
Tanguero,
tango on…

2

Sparrow of sentences
popping up under the bushes
pecking at the ground of this and that…

Landing in Miami I hear you everywhere,
pero, pero, pero, the *pero* Cubano, the *pero*
of Nueva York

And at midnight mounting my last flight to Argentina
I hear the smallest *pero* of all, the one that lives in my heart still
pecking: *pero, pero, pero* what if when I finally arrive he is no
longer there…

A Poem of Home Waits

There it assembles itself
brick by brick like the house
my father built only it seems
older and smaller, the little girl
who peeked out of the upstairs window

grown large, unwieldy, standing
in a black raincoat at the bottom
of the front steps. Should it snow she could never
roll down this front lawn now but, some consolation,
she can hear the symphony of the old elm tree as it yellows
sends its leaves quivering through the wet air…

Just there behind the stiff gray-and-white
striped draperies where merry-go-round horses
pranced on the polished cotton—the room she dreamt in
for ten solid years, the hands that braided her hair
married to the voice that taught her to repeat the twelve
Hebrew words she whispered each day upon arising

"Did u knock on the door?" texts Arthur from his smart
phone. "No, I always was a shy child, and the taxi was
waiting…"

And so waits the poem, its little blue eyes closed on its
childhood bed, for its own future to walk down the three
bottom steps and, tears caught in its throat, fold itself back
into the black Twin City's Cab with a driver from Somalia
whisking it away through the streets of St. Paul

Footfalls, March 2015

On a rock high above me
a turkey vulture stood
on tippy toes drying
its huge outspread wings

While below on the trail
I heard my own footfalls
one after another, my two-legged
creature out of a Sunday in search of beauty.
'Twas a dull day in the country,
as if a veil had been flung
over bush, tree, and rock, over scampering
creatures, birdcalls, and the ponds standing still
without glitter as past the flat meadows my feet
clomped along falling into time with me, my day
waning as my night had waned

Try as I would,
sing as I would, pray as I would, the earth could not
come forth to meet me but as I returned to the
trailhead to leave where I began there was the thing of
beauty standing still, spreading its wings in the sunlight
to dry.

On Leaving the Academy of Science

January 25, 2015

My 73rd birthday and on our visit here
the Planetarium had a special show about
what will happen to my body after you
bury me, exactly:

How it will break down into its elements
the little creatures that will come busting
into the wicker casket and take what they
want of me for supper

And how I will migrate into the sparkly rhizomes
and travel up into the roots of the great trees
above me their leaves falling down, my poems.

A butterfly, a *California Sister,* lit on my hand at the top of
the Academy of Science in the bird and butterfly jungle.
I saw her marvelous tongue uncurl,
surrendered myself to the next generation of poets. She licked
each of my cuticles, flitted over to Sophie and landed on her
flowered headband awhile, then swooped back to me suddenly
landing on my nose. We all took pictures with her there, she,
glued to the spot. No voice or movement unsettled her. *On the
nose, Poet. If you only have one day left, say what you must say
but make it winged. Do what you must do, but make it fly!*

We left The Academy of Science at twilight.
You, my children, grandchildren walked ahead
to the strains of the guitar being strummed out in the park.
I was behind you, watching you move on, into the night.

II. The Butterfly Blouse—2016

The Butterfly Blouse

There you are at Reouven's bar mitzvah in a translucent blouse appliquéd in multicolored butterflies, long pearls hanging over the black silk shell Amy stitched up for you right before we flew

And here *we* are, all in one long printed line, great-grandson, granddaughter, you, and me, your oldest daughter, the one writing all of this down

You turned a dazzling smile toward the camera as you stood with Reouven in that party hall in Paris where minutes later you and I trudged through the sea of black-hatted men (seated separately from the women, of course) to reach the one and only bathroom in the place

I know you wanted the perfect orthodox burial, Mother, the little white shroud like a space suit all buttoned up, folded over you, and the white bonnet tied just so

But at the last moment I had to send them to accompany you the bright, winged ones trapped in your gauzy blouse straight from that last *simcha*

"Yes, it's done!" winked the attendant from Desert Memorial Park, used to many such bizarre requests

So that here I may sit years later among softly rustling trees and imagine their wings carrying you breast heart shoulders flutter fluttering through that sea of black hats

All the way home…

Two from Lufthansa

1. Sleep over Germany

An hour at most
but deep and swimming
in the dark plane

in the body of my mother
so that when I awake I have to
rush past rows of the mute
closed faces toward the spacious
silver john…

Down the stairway of the jumbo jet
swishing past stars and the two little doors
swinging behind me.
Groggy, stiff necked and filled
with sadness the kind only she knew,
her own world almost vanished
her arrival time unforeseen and cloaked
with fear.

2. Smoking Chamber

Munich.
To the right of Gate G19, a square Plexiglass-sealed room. "Smoking" the sign says. And there, under a blue light, like a cageful of rare animals, the Smokers, in transit, lighting up. Quietly. Puffing. Inhaling each other's exhale. Nowhere to sit so they do it standing. Does it alarm you that to this point this prose has no poem in it?

But show me forbiddenness and I'll show you a poem as two of them face each other in short perky haircuts, connect, begin to kiss, their lungs turning pink under their slinky sweaters, their low-slung jeans allowing their navels to escape and float upward, their cigarettes thudding to the floor unsmoked in a single pristine pack. Green, hip, good for the planet, the longer they kiss the steamier the chamber becomes. Other smokers have trouble lighting up. Some actually leave. The eco-revolutionists prolong their activism without even coming up for air while plane after plane takes off into the velvet night.

While star after star spins.

Your Art in Times of Sadness

for Agneta Falk on her 70th

Like a fashion shoot. The runway—a Central European air terminal and this is the latest: two torsos ripped by the blast exposing bare skin, undergarments, ashes over jeans worn with heels ripped off, one woman holding a cell phone in her red hand trying to connect

Now add two left hands gloved in black to hide the explosive detonators caught on the overhead monitor blood-streaked faces the sound of wailing alternating with shocky silence before the shriek of sirens arriving just one day before I shuffle toward my own jet home from my French family as they trudge through the streets of Paris, moving targets fanning out from Gare du Nord closed and emptied today for a bomb threat

The sky blazes for me opening my heart like one of your brilliant paintings as the closely watched trains of your latest poem move ever so slowly through the landscape below…

3/27/16

Waving

A wave is a wave, but at the same time it is water.
—Thich Nhat Hahh

One of us is on the ship, one on the shore...
So we wave, we wave furiously, the distance increases furiously, we wave, the distance decreases, we wave and wave, it looks like the ship will come close enough so that you can land, jump off, run up to me, or I can jump into the water, swim out and climb up on board, slipping and shivering but, oh, something is going on at the cellular level, the molecular level, the atomic level, we realize that the water in you is continuous with the water between us and in me and we wave furiously so furiously that blip, blop, slip, slop, we become the boat, the water, the eternal shore...

12/20/15
for Elyam (The Sea) Raz Winnick

The Great Bliss Queen Meets Omar

She comes with her arms spread wide in her cloak, the cloak I stitched for her, my cloth of coral cotton centered by a rose of gold

With arms spread wide she swoops down over Omar
for his final hug

Just a man, a hero who loaded his trucks with food and medicine, watched over by drones from above with their searing eyes

Out of his bombed convoy his hand waving from his shrapnel-pocked body to the White Helmets to come get him, but after a second strafing, "We had to leave Omar," they said. "We hid ourselves in a truck that wasn't burning. It was loaded with flour; we thought this could protect us."

Flowering flour. #US Style claim the Syrians, claim the Russians. *Hashtag.* A word for the ground meat of an utterance gone ballistic. Go. Read all of your hashtags and counter hashtags. And weep for the flowering of the Great Bliss Queen over an aid convoy bound to Aleppo taking into her furious arms the soul of Omar Barakat, who helped all the poor and displaced and refugees, leaving behind no one who could be who he was, know what he knew, smile what he smiled, plan what he planned, love whom he loved, his eyes wide open always to what he was called to do.

Gathered into her blazing arms because he knew what he knew, her bliss as a quality of his mind centering himself in the vortex swept up into the blinding mineral seeds of hope in her white silence, white light the poor battle-scarred earth grinding beneath them of our primal human
delusions.

9/20/16 for Aleppo

The Compliment

"There's always a staircase by a river," said my father
growing younger and younger a star in each eye as
my grandmother mounted even higher in her huge black hat.
I complained to them that you never tell me I'm pretty.
"You're stunning," said my father in the pale whistle-y voice
of someone very far away.

Seven Bathers in the Garden of Victoria Ocampo

What are these school children to think being herded through bedrooms papered with old photographs in the summer house of Victoria Ocampo?

In their white uniforms they ponder the poet sitting in a car, scandalous for her time, cigarette dangling from her lipsticked mouth, and certain faces painted as they were by the mad wind into her upstairs windows.

As these children traipse through her copious garden they spy seven robins bathing as always in her generous waters…

And what does their Maestra have to say about this writer's passions and the pen that sought to redeem them as fresh light was hurled in through these very windows from the Atlantic?

The children pass through the house in white uniforms, their unwritten sighs, their songs yet to be sung, their wings curled up tight as buttons.

11/24/17
Mar del Plata, Argentina

On Not Being Recognized

There was a famous writer floating nearby, and his wife.
They were meeting with their literary agent.

Even here! The game is never over. She was guiding them
through a series of deadlines. Even here…

As I floated on my back in the water I could see
the sun moving through a funnel of clouds. I tried
to rise up, but a heavy mass at the back of my
neck, my very own hair grown wild and long,
first had to be lifted out of the water and rung dry.

My father was larger than I remembered and very
muscular, what's known as "a heavy lifter."

"Wow!" I uttered, impressed as he hefted a pure
glass coffee table and replaced it in a new location.

"At first we didn't recognize you," he began in his
husky, urgent voice. It looked like some old thing
just floating on the water…

"I was so tired," I said.
"Well, I slept very well last night," he responded,
"and you will, too."

"What did he mean?" I thought, as the whole scene
cut out like an old movie. "And why didn't my
own father recognize me?"

Man in Bed with Me

I turn

And there
in the place I am
reserving for you
should you ever get here
is *he* instead, a being so still
eyes so closed body so washed
so clean, so not breathing…

On what wind
in which of night's envelopes
has this cold Islander come?

After my morning prayers I send
money to those he has left behind
and that day when I bake, roll, bless
my bread, I will it into the closed
bakery blown to bits in dark waves
that once fed his family,

and into the raging rain-swollen earth
to feed his strangled kingdom.

10/16/16
for Haiti

I Saw the President Dance

I saw the President dance, sounding that gentle voice in which he skims over sorrow. The police were listening, the Black Lives Matter were listening, and the public, we, were listening too. In weary tones he tried many things, with his head bent, tried the dance of the truth as he saw it gliding over our grief the way those high birds turn on winds among clouds. He did not weep, nor did he accuse, tho' it was a time for both weeping and accusing, but like a whirling many-sided being his arms flung wide he did the truth dance so lightly, so gravely, embracing his America, the one he serves as the small single light blazes among dark windows, the sun rising at last over painful dawns, the quiet sad dance of all he knows and tries to be, the one man failing, rising, failing-again dance, the many-colored dance of the multitudes that we are, the gun dance, the nuclear weapon dance, the falling to earth dance, the rising in smoke dance, the scared little children dance, the little children dying dance, the big men scared and flying killing and dying dance, the women scared, strangled raped and dying, killing and dying dance, the black dance, the white dance, the all he knows, is, will ever be dance. The dance of the fields of sunflowers as they all face the same direction, blooming, bowing, bursting forth their seeds and withering to the ground dance, the gourd dance, the star dance, the Grand Canyon dance and the dance of the great waterfall that made the Grand Canyon dance, the dance Scripture made when it was scribed dance, the dance of himself, the President, the dance of his single breath, his dance.

And then the chorus played and sang "The Battle Hymn of The Republic," and the five faces of the dead police stared out of their photographs and the living embraced the living, and it all went blank, and all of us, the police, the Black Lives Matter, and we, the public, all of us went home.

7/12/16
Dallas, Texas

III. The Tree of Wheat—2017

Rabbi Yehuda and the Tree of Wheat

for David Meltzer

These things were imagined long before they were thought
long before they were said, so he pulled this out of his sack
of dreams saying to the others "Wheat is a tree,"

as they sat at their work under a *Gemara*-colored
sky. They wanted to see into Paradise, seeking to discover
together what tree it was whereof ate Eve and tempted Adam.

"Figs," said one remembering how the first couple
had covered their nakedness with fig leaves.

"Grapes," said another remembering the drunkenness of Noah…

But Rabbi Yehuda with a star in each eye asked "How do we
know 'tree'?" His voice was light, bubbly, transcendent, mystical,
humorous, like your voice, David. And he went that one step
further than either of them, seeing a place low and dusty with his
own gritty ancestors wandering against the whirling wind.

No tall verticals crowned with leafy boughs for him, no round
fruit dropping down to tantalize. "It was wheat," he said, once
more hearing a snicker perhaps from the others, and added
somewhat slyly, "The baby does not know how to cry
father, mother, until he tastes the taste of grain."

Enigmatic. Like you, David. May we all partake of the grain
sprouting from your tree and learn to cry into the hiddenness
with wild gentleness, with rippling laughter.

Together may we reach your farthest shore…

Binyamin the Shepherd and I

I'm paging the thicket of teachings
on the subject of blessing my food:
The categories
The dictates
The nuances
surrounding the correct blessing
of the origin of the bite about to be taken
This bite
of baked apple with yogurt and walnuts
sprinkled with cinnamon
deep in the future world of this cluster
of Talmudic rabbis
This bite in my present world
what they struggle to pair with the divine force
which created it, assembling its molecules
through time and space channeling them thru
tree, cow, and plant thru delivery systems
feeding into the Good Earth Market, Fairfax, California
and thru me, shopping bag in hand, whisking me into apple
dairy nut space, debit card in hand…

Who gave me the oven to bake the apple in
and the bowl to plop it into?
And the wherewithal to slather it with Greek
yogurt, top it with aforementioned ingredients?
Who will watch over me so I don't choke
as I spoon it into my gullet?
Who keeps me breathing evenly as I eat it
and what are the specific attributes of this
Divine being and which of those should be mentioned
before this bite be taken?
Must we not bring

all of this into consciousness before
(pause here with slightly closed eyes)
we eat? The rabbis of the Talmud most certainly
did. But the scholars mention one Binyamin the Shepherd
who after gobbling up his lunch as I always do was suddenly hit
with the urge to bless. Sitting on a rock in the sun a few crumbs
drifting down the front of his coarse linen
his belly stilled for an instant from its eternal rumble
lifting his face to the sky he simply shouts out, "Bless
the Master of this bread!"

Why Rav Adda bar Ahava Stood on the Banks of the Dannak River

for Adin Steinsaltz

The river flowing in their ears
the great Rav's students were seated
on the banks of the Dannak River
returning from his funeral.
"Let us go and eat bread,"
they had vowed. A sad meal,
a holy meal, a shared meal.
The river flowing in their ears.
After they ate, they sat and raised
a dilemma about their meal
not in their capability to resolve.

Rav Adda bar Ahavah stood

the river flowing in his ears
in all of their ears.
It is said that he rent his
garment a second time.
It is said that he remarked,
"Rav is dead, and we have not yet learned…"
But this is not why he stood, the river flowing
in his ears, in their ears.
A great and mysterious soul
was about to pass among them. A learned
soul, who would teach them exactly what
they needed to know.

Rav Adda bar Ahava rose in order to honor
the soul of this great teacher.

Big Cloud, Little Cloud

My Aunt Irene died pregnant after a car crash
her dark stars rearranging themselves as Grandma's
hair turned white overnight and her youngest refused
to eat for a year. My mother named me after her soft-eyed
sister once photographed with her finger-waved brown bob
walking down a flight of stairs in a jaunty suit,
high heels, marrying a man no one liked, a man who
disappeared after the crash and was never again glimpsed

in the family album. Grandma would stand washing
dishes at the sink in our cottage on Big Floyd Lake,
short red gingham curtains blowing against the
screened kitchen windows, humming

> *Good Night, Irene,*
> *Good Night, Irene.*
> *Good night, Irene, Sleep tight, Irene,*
> *I'll see you in my dreams.*

I was born the oldest grandchild, but one went before me
with Irene. Little planet, little August rose, long-ago grace
note to my first cry. The LAPD pulled me over in my own
ninth month, speeding home and timing my contractions.
When the two officers saw my condition they waved me on, "Be
careful, Ma'am," all they said. What if they had known? I like to
think they rearranged some stars that day, my first born blue and
needing to be resuscitated, Irene watching.

They're all in the room at a birth, you know, my aunt making sure
we were all right before she flew, big cloud, little cloud, I love
you.

From a Letter to Rilke

And she comes flitting at the side of my car, my mother,
dressed in a lavender sweater and that cap she bought on
her last cruise. "Monarch of the Seas" it proclaims, doubles her
meaning. Queen or butterfly? I think more the latter as she goes
back and forth pressing for an instant her blissful smile
against the glass then away only to return once more, full
blue-gray of her eyes full pink of her lips so young as I sat in my
blue time capsule…
Dying she said, "You will be in charge of me in my carriage,"
and I loved her moving back that way, isn't death so formal amid
those cathedrals of yours, in Naples and Rome…

But I am come down to your poem to ask you a different
question: "Who are you in the end who stood right next to your
pages a blond phantom, red-and-green-plaid-shirt, so tall you
were in my little house, then darkening, with one of my coffee
cups in your hand? Cupboard-love loyalty of which you wrote
(through your translators of course) yet this particular cup
you held in your hand bore a small glazed butterfly…
and your eyes fixed on the distance, why were they smiling?"

And tell me, is my small poetry in vain? No, not yours, of course,
which you heard and sang between violin and rose drenched sea-
storm, but Rainer, there she is again, almost taunting me, her
cheek against the glass…

Como Tu

for Javier Zamora

"Now you know somebody, now go do something," you say before reading to a large crowd on YouTube every day. Could they see the poem tattooed into you under your shirt and jacket, the one where your countryman, Roque Dalton, says that his veins don't end in himself but are part of everyone who loves what he does. What if they don't? Could you love them even then? You have followed your young veins all the way across the Sonoran Desert to your peril, and to this very room. And out of them, one by one, the prized poems emerge. We gasp, weep, sigh, clap for each one. We lay down cash for your books. You ask that we pray for you on your journey back to your Grandmother's kitchen. *Como Tu.* We all have grandmothers. *Como tu* we are struggling to return to them. Will you pray for us as well?

For Sharon Doubiago on the 5th of July

My house, wherever it has been in this life, has had an extra window since that day in 1982 when you signed for me your poem "Hard Country." Here it is now on the bedroom wall, clipped behind glass, looking toward a sun-drenched prairie.

And here, now, the woman still waiting for her death, caught in her timeless reflections, her vision lighting the poem from within, a most perfect melding of person, place, history, and myth, these thirty-five-year passing between you and me, turning, continuing through the rivered sweep of Earth, the old house rearranging itself time and again under its ancient cottonwood tree.

And as I sat yesterday in the silence of a midsummer California night following the faint boom of fireworks at the county fair, I thought, "Now the Fair is over," the prizes awarded, musicians have jammed, pigs have run their races, and the poets have read their poems, words drowned out by the infamous Cyclone as it roared past them. Just then, as the day with its prizes ended, it came into my heart to tell you what you have meant to me. You, burning through your life, a blond comet, your unceasing intellect moving over your story, learning as you mounted each place on our planet's starry map how to articulate the earth's messages, braid them with your own, pull the strands tight, and coil them into coronas of ecstatic knowing. In you I was forever challenged to go deeper, think larger, un-chart the waters, make them my own. You grew into your own great westward movement, a strong-willed eager-limbed girl of a Whitman making our land forever your own.

And as the sun rose on the 5th of July this morning I saw it rise into your eyes, Sharon, with a sun dance winding itself around the sacred pole of a cottonwood tree, surrounded by native peoples, exhausted, bleeding into their wristlets and crowns of sage, their breath moving through the piping

wing bones of eagles in their annual ordeal to save the earth. To redeem the earth, you've caught what flies and made it sing. Suffering, you've unearthed the unearthable, striking out on your lone voyages time after time in your blue van, the windshield carrying like windblown leaves a first line, a poem title, an image, you rolling with them down a new road, an old street.

My house, wherever it has been in this life, has been blessed by an extra window, where the light and the sound of my own prairie's rush into its multiple horizons could be thought out and whispered, seen and heard, keenly felt, and clearly loved, by the grace of you, your words continually returning me to all that is solid, mysterious, and true.

Peanut-Butter-and-Jellies

for Kharon Davis

Today we're in Alabama with you who were charged with murder ten years ago. Two judges four teams of lawyers and nine trial dates later (the district attorney who charged you long retired) you have not yet had your speedy trial, the opposite, and languishing in jail who could blame you when the craving for something simple, innocent, overtook you. You wanted peanut-butter-and-jelly sandwiches. Wanted to sink your teeth into that state of innocence before cold milk would wash them down your throat. So you procured them, a couple of unauthorized peanut-butter-and-jellies, and for this, and the fighting that accompanies such hostile acts, you were put in solitary.

Through it all you maintain you are innocent of murder as charged, but for the past two nights now unknowingly in solidarity with you, I, too, have partaken of peanut-butter-and-jellies and like Clarice Lispector's heroine in *The Passion According to C.H.* have actually thought, "Though, as for my desires, my passions, my contact with a tree—they are still for me like a mouth, eating." And after all of this eating I am compelled to report:

Whether you killed the man or not, I know not what should happen to you and I hope, since this is a small town, that I'm not, at last, on the jury. But it was wrong that they locked you in solitary for eating the unauthorized peanut-butter-and-jellies. They do the same, all the time, I know it, as I, myself, do it, and it was dead wrong.

But let us be clear: Lispector's heroine murdered that cockroach before she ate it. And that was Brazil, not Alabama. The same laws do not apply.

Simple Math

Any other schoolboy could understand this, you
in your suit and tie talking gloriously around
it for one hour. The poverty, the fallen, the shot dead
crawling up on the sidewalk next to your newly shined shoes.

Any other schoolboy with his thatch of red-blond hair plastered
over his forehead could get this. Simple math. You are super rich,
figure it out. How come they're crawling around down there like
ants without stock accounts? How come they've been shot dead?

Don't give me the La La Land speech, where you parade around
with your ravishing partner, our future brilliant as a Maxfield
Parrish.

Any other kid could figure this one out.

IV. Paper Dolls—2018

Paper Dolls

for Brooke Goffstein

"God lost interest in people ages ago and now is just happy with a paper-doll collection," you once expressed, but no one reading these words can understand how God's happiness could ever be so bound up in this sunlight on green carpet, two cousins, all the time in the world coursing thru their child bodies, scissors, paper, colored pencils and crayons only, producing such lasting joy.

You a six-year-old teacher to five-year-old me as we sat, intent, to draw the little white bodies, to design what they would wear. Most important: the dolls were children. Square feet, chubby hands, red mouths, tiny clear eyes. I don't remember a lot of giggling or fits of temper. No one was torn up or crumpled into waste. Our work was serious, as any act of love, our colors pure, our lines, true. God loved us doing it, and, a little jealous, perhaps, turned his back on even Harry S. Truman just to watch.

And so, I like to think, my brilliant cousin, that when your time came on the very winter day of your birth, God reached God's hand to lift you, bent the rain-bowed light just so to garment your frail shoulders, let your sleeves blow long and loose, and clipped a final hem at your white feet. "I'm not going to give her shoes today," the voice of a child could be heard to say,

"Let her squish the grass between her toes. Let her run free…"

2/12/18

From a Letter to Rilke, #2

And what if walking on the beach no angelic voice calls out to me? Ever. I'm so much older than you were now. If it were going to happen, they would have contacted me by this hour, I think. But today I did call out, "Angela, Angela!" so my voice could be heard over the surf. And she answered, "I didn't recognize you!" What would you do then? What would you think if the Angel were a real person, born in London, so that whatever she says in her warm British voice makes one think of tea and cream and buttered scones? Angela, in a black parka buttoned up against the wind and her gold hoop earrings glittering against the ground fog and sea mist, crash! Another wave, and we speak of this and that, time and death working their way into the conversation, Rainer, but here is the thing: someone came before us to this spot on the beach, early this morning, and built a perfect sandcastle, complete with an arch, and many pointed turrets. I don't know how/what holds it all up, and as we are taking it in, a young woman comes toward us with a 9-week-old puppy, a bull terrier, and there you are, your big eyes staring at the tiny creature who walks bravely up to Angela's large collie mix four times the little one's size, and your big eyes staring at the two of them, you breathe in and out, the tiny white chest of the terrier, no bigger than a sea gull's breast with its bull-doggy face hanging over it, little black ring around the left eye looks up at—Rainer Maria Rilke! And God only knows what he sees, crash! Another wave until the young woman with very perfect breasts bends before your large eyes and lifts her puppy to her warm gray sweater. Did you think about that when you went back home to your desk to pay some bills, and about the woman who answered when I called, "Angela!" and all of the waves before and after crashing, the castle by that time completely gone, and Angela taking out her golden earrings in the nightly dark and folding herself into her covers rocked by the midnight sea?

On Eating Walleye Pike at the St. Paul Grill

These are *farmed,* Grandpa,
something you could never have imagined
as you sat patiently chewing on the stump
of a cold cigar, straw fishing hat squished down
over your bald head. "There's Old Man Diamond,"
Daddy would tease, as you sat waiting for
the solitary-as-you-were walleye pike as he
swirled at the bottom of Big Floyd Lake.

They cooked it in *pecans and maple syrup,*
Grandma, a taste you could never imagine, as you stood
aproned, the red gingham curtains behind you and that
old toilet that ran all the time as background music
and you shook the fresh caught fish in your brown
paper bag of Bisquick and laid them lovingly in the
sputtering pan over sliced onions. Crispy, the slightly
dark parts of their flesh a hint of the deep shadows of
the lake's underworld from which they were drawn…

Farmed? Pecans and maple syrup? Did I fly two
thousand miles for this? No rhubarb crisp on the menu,
no canasta duels deep into the night betwixt the two of
you, the lamp over the oilcloth-clad kitchen table
swinging gently, circling your nightly playing field. All
of this I had for ten summers in our perverse and war-
torn world and was never asked to pay the bill.

One Sunday Afternoon

for Susan Griffin

Green how I want you green
sings out Susan in the midst
of the overstuffed furniture
in the midst of the spilled champagne
and the glitter of eyeglasses
and all of our haunches planted
on the white folding chairs
and the stuffed eggs stiffening
at the edge of the bright lawn
marked with strange little divots
and bright little flags...

And Kathy leans over to me
after the last line has died,
whispers, "I saw a house once
outside of Granada. They took him
from there and had him shot
on the grounds near an ancient fountain..."

We stare into each other's eyes
poet-to-poet, purses flat on the floor
at our feet, reminded in an instant
how the poem and death keep such
intimate company just as our current
head of state begins to tether gender absolutely
back to birth certificate, just as our current head of state prepares
his welcoming committee for the migrants now marching north
across Mexico.
García Lorca of the fierce black brow trembling
among us and the champagne turning
to blood (what else is champagne for?)

and today's fund raisers counting their take
as we poets glide out into the garden once more
Green how I want you green
as the little boats below strain
at their tethers over the blue bay
and in another country a woman weeps
for her love who walked into a Saudi
Embassy not long ago for papers to marry
and they did to this journalist
what they once did to Federico García Lorca.

Poem on the Earth Moving South

1.

How we forget in the midst of living
the creature upon which we live and die
curved and green
wave on wave of hills
turning under wide blue
leaf and grain
and moss and grass bearing.
Temperate and frigid
she stirs in her sleep,
rumbles awake, underling
of vast planetary space
keeping our place
and though we dance and drill
drive and flame
she can embrace
water and time
those two strangers that run
through our fingers like sand

2.

Fields of cloud
far as my eyes can see
uninterrupted by treetops
or ceilings
cherubs or falling angels
of red, yellow, blue

"Look, Love,
The *Cordillera de Los Andes*,"
you said in a snow-covered voice

"Look up at those high peaks, Mom,"
you said in awe as we flew alongside
the Himalayas.

We could rave and wonder
with patient airports waiting below
in sparkling beads of electric light
the pull of the earth upon which they are strung
has yet to fail us.

3.

Zipping my white rental car
thru endless desert at dusk,
the white campers nestling into dunes
solitary
parked far from one another

My father, the self-proclaimed desert rat at my side,
my mother within me after I visited
their two little houses side by side at last.

"Look who's here, so beautiful!"
I cried out as I saw the still-white letters on her
grave; a meeting of sorts, grief-filled
She could have said that to me, as well, did say it:
"You and your mother are on a journey together.
And it has to do with your writing!"

4.

However slowly she turns
be it in light or in dark
However she suffers us
as her great disturbance, nothing more,
we earthlings in our transient knowing,
in our tiny cars of metal…in the midst of our living,
how we forget.

3/18/18
Anza Borrego, California

Rabbi Tweeting the Un-Tweetable

in memory of Mireille Knoll
March 23, 2018

Here's what it's come to:
Mireille Knoll, having been knifed 11 times and burned in her apartment because she was a Jew with her post-Holocaust body, and the terror she endured at the end of her 85-year-old life, has created a tweetable event.
And the tweeter? The Head Rabbi of Paris.

Isn't there written somewhere in the Holiness Code
a prohibition against reducing an act so grave into those requisite 280 characters? Where are the great Hebrew poets, the cantors in their tall hats with the sobs in their throats wrapped around notes that rise up into low-hanging clouds to push them on toward the great dropping ear locks of the Holy One? And is there no scribe left who dipping himself in cool waters to self-purify, no one scribe who will coat his quill (sharpened with the holiest blade) coat it with the blackest of ink to honor the body of this woman whose great great great grandparents lay in splendor somewhere, under stars we can barely imagine, throbbing to create one letter in one name that would turn in its generative power, come down into the body of one Mireille, child fleeing Paris, her small hand in the palm of her Brazilian mother, to escape the inescapable hatred that finally ended her life rooted, as it is, in our existential Jewish burial candle cry?

Prayer to Be Said on Entering an American Synagogue

Here I am again, God of my Fathers and my Mothers
in my customary place up front facing the piano, the heavy
blue book of prayers in my hands, and with me my joy, my pain,
my grateful heart, and most of all, my eternal questions!

Should I be shot down by an agitated hate-filled countryman, will you hold those I leave behind tenderly as I would have? Tell my children, my grandchildren, my great grandchildren it was my deep desire to be here among the Hebrew prayers and songs that have comforted me and guided me as much as I desire, always, to be with them in times of joy and sorrow. Carry them, I pray, to a place where they can see the gift of my life and give them peace. Then do this for all the bereaved in Squirrel Hill tonight as I stand, Oh, God of my Fathers and Mothers, in this place for them…

10/28/18

The Cigar of Fidel

For an instant
the horse poised
on the hill
happiness being the horse
human rights being the hill.
Fidel Castro has come to Chile
for the inauguration of Salvador Allende

And Fidel is smiling,
in his breast pocket
three Cuban cigars

The Argentines, well loved
because they have produced
Ché, are given prime seats
at the inauguration of Allende
and an interview with Fidel

You know how men clap each other
on the shoulder?

I am picturing Fidel clapping Marcelo
on his shoulder after he has asked: "Are these
the famous Cuban cigars made especially
for you?"
Fidel smiles
Happiness *is* on the hill for an instant
and Fidel takes a cigar from his breast
pocket and gives it to Marcelo.
Of such small incidents History
is composed. Marcelo, although he doesn't
smoke, taking the cigar
thanking Fidel.

Let's say universal health care
is a human right
and is rolled up
in the brown paper.
Marcelo, when he returns to Argentina,
wraps the cigar and secretes it
in the depths of an attaché case.

Allende is assassinated.
The elegant horse
falling, falling from its moment
on the crest of the greenest hill.

What happens to this small souvenir of brief
happiness? It lies in the dark in an attaché case.
Marcelo doesn't smoke and not being in a position
of power in his own country, the cigar is not passed
on with a clap on the shoulder to someone else.
The crime rate continues to climb in Argentina.
Then on Marcelo's 64th birthday, which he is spending at the
Fairmont Hotel in San Francisco,
a message from a neighbor: his apartment has been *ocupado* by a
gang of thugs. He flies home, calls the police, and clears the
apartment, now cleaned out of all valuables, photograph files,
memorabilia, his dead wife's clothes. What did the *ocupas* do
with the souvenir of the moment of happiness from the pocket of
Fidel Castro? Pawing through the attaché case and being
apolitical as thugs are wont to be (Wait. Hold that thought. We
will examine it in its entirety and all of its ramifications when we
look back at our own last election.)

Was the Havana cigar of Fidel tossed into the garbage? Or did one
ocupa unroll the paper, take the now-stale moment of happiness

wrapped around universal healthcare and labeled with two white bands, the first saying COHIBA, the second saying FIDEL CASTRO in black, easy to read, and roll it between his thumb and two fingers maybe holding it up to his fellow-thugs and say, "Anyone want a puff of a stale Cuban cigar?" Then maybe they laughed the *ocupa* laugh, not having an inkling, a clue, as to what this is all about.

Clair de Lune

She is last to play in a field of ten, three judges tabled before the baby grand piano, and, past the immediate curtain of pure tension, hanging ivy is moving against the wall of windows through which can be seen, far-off, a man calmly seated on a stone ledge, his back to us and facing an expanse of the light-soaked San Francisco Bay.

She executes a crisp bow in black suit and floral tie, cuffs rolled back over jacket sleeves, presenting her small hands to the gleaming keys. A moment of silence to connect with the spirit of the composer, a sharp intake of breath, a whispered "Now!" and Claude Debussy fills the room, presses against the church windows, the rustling leaves fluttering against them, beyond the wide water, trembling. My mother, who has been gone five years now, soars into the room in cream flannel, coral roses on wings of a moonlit sadness, the music now pouring out of the black instrument at the touch of her great-granddaughter's hands.

The man begins to levitate slightly off the wall of stones, the water before him crashing in green waves against an invisible shore. There is perfume in the air, a faraway look as the sapphire eyes of the piano player search the invisible shore, the gleaming shore, threshold, majesty, a small golden crown settling into her short blond hair as great-grandmother circles, circles above her in the moonlight, cream flannel, coral roses, and slowly vanishes…the man is high over the water now, he lifts one hand, palm open toward the glittering light-soaked bay above which a blue moon has slowly risen! Ah! His favorite perfume, and we can smell it…

Poem in Which I Dream I Am the Newly Elected President of Mexico

Long involved dream.
The essence: I am now López Obrador. I have new shoes, the exact color of the clay of Mexican soil. In them I must now ride a bicycle through the jungles of my country. I am managing, but my left foot keeps slipping off the pedal. I have to ride the road wedged between two large trucks, gray in color. One is depression, economic and personal. The second is repression. Political. Cool jungle-y trees arch overhead to keep the blazing sun at bay for the moment as I figure this out. My right foot starts giving me problems now. How can I keep it inside my shoe as my nation's state-run oil company continually conflates it with severe problems of corruption and inefficiency? I have a certain momentum, however. The way is dark and cool for the moment. But my left foot keeps slipping off the pedal. Under these conditions, how can I progress? Periodically, brilliant birds emerge from the canopy high above, their wings as far from me as the hopes of the people who brought this bike to me and said, simply, "Now, López Obrador, *you* ride!"

For Prosper in Jerusalem

Across the miles I am with you as your plane lands
at Ben Gurion and once more you travel up to Jerusalem
for your funeral tomorrow.

Your son and grandson will speak the words their hearts are
forming tonight and the rabbis will accompany your still form
into the ancient and contested soil of our people. But tonight I am
remembering the night our children were wed! Dapper and
humorous, your dark soft eyes sparkling, you presented your arm
to me. We left the *chuppah,* now related, that the beautiful new
marriage born of us would give untold joy. You were to be the one
near to them. I was to be the one far away.

And the first time I crossed the skies to visit them, you and
Rachel prepared a light supper for me. We sat in your kitchen,
you, so at ease and kind. It was winter. You offered me your
specialty: fresh fruit, hand-picked from stalls at the Paris markets.
Huge grapes from Italy tasting like perfume, lychees from the
south of China. I had never eaten them fresh, and you peeled the
cinnamon swirl away to reveal, voila! the silky white fruit inside.
And after you poured your special tea of fresh mint leaves and
honey into little glasses we stumbled through a conversation:
a little English, a little French, reinforced by *Español* and *Ivrit.*
We began on a road of many happinesses, only marred by this one
great sadness at the end.

V. If a Star Could Talk—2019

If a Star Could Talk

for Natasha and Seth Amitin

It would flash a smile
as did the small boy sipping
a chocolate milk in Buttonwillow,
California, at the local Starbucks
he destined north on Highway 5
I destined south, neither of us
staring into cellphones, computers

If a star could talk it would glisten out of the black
5 a.m. sky as the Beatles sing "Love, Love, Love"
and I hop into my Subaru and make it on down
thru LA to Palm Springs, as the star points from
its high road above my road telling me to get to
that family wedding and to bring the others along,
if a star could talk, could dance again, could sing…

For Aliza, Born in December

Years before your father was born I hiked to a high place in the Sierra Nevada. Freezing cold, little baby. Few midget trees clinging to rocks. Years before your grandmother married your grandfather, even. Back then. I laid my head down under ringing stars, Aliza, and I slept. I dreamt of my own father's voice. There in the palm of his hand, which he was holding out to me, was a large, bright orange. Then I climbed down from that high place, took up my pen and wrote, "My Father and the Fruit of Paradise."

Now you have one of those fathers! Who each day must climb to a very high place, under ringing stars, to give thanks for you who came to him mid-winter, from that garden we only see in dreams.

The oranges in my California yard are shivering in their bright jackets under freezing rain today, while *you* are sunbathing in Miami! May you grow strong and a little wild. May you climb to a very high place and converse with me, your own great-grandmother, someday, under the ringing stars…

Many years after the dream, a man unwrapped its meaning for me. It was a casual conversation. I was buying a bunch of yellow daisies from him. "We were so poor in those shtetls. But whenever we knew someone was about to die we pooled our few coins. We bought that person a bright orange."

"Why?" I asked him.
Aliza, you must always ask, "Why?"
"So that man, that woman could taste something," said the man, as he wrapped up the bouquet of yellow daisies I had purchased, "from the World to Come. So that man, that woman, shouldn't be afraid."

1/18/20

"Lenski's Aria" on the Lips of My Granddaughter

for Maya

Silver flute studded with mysterious keys
your long rosy fingers delicately traveling
its royal spine

Large serious eyes gazing into the audience
but beyond to where the ill-fated Lenski stands
in a crisp white shirt and black tuxedo
lamenting the loss of his golden spring times

You bare his tragic sadness with your young breath
echoing his sigh, his deep love, his death, your black-clad form
standing onstage, a little sideways now so we can almost see the
Russian graveyard, the mass of dark trees behind you evoking the
wind as it bursts from Lenski's soul, his lament becoming you as
you reach toward his cries with your outstretched arms, your lithe
figure containing the torrent…

Last night you deeply slept, the pounded rain,
the thundered lightning, to fill yourself with enough storming to
become this Russian poet, breathing him into us now with silver
studded agony —*Where, oh where, have you gone,*
      my golden springs?

as slowly you allow his question to die on the silent-ing air…

5/19/19

Bye Bye Blackbird

In the last days you seemed younger, flamboyant,
dashing around the halls in your wheelchair
at Desert Hospital in that cherry blossom print
kimono I found for you with your favorite caregiver,
a young Filipino nurse, who, after you were
deeply attached to him, left suddenly for a better job.

"Bye, bye, Blackbird," you sang out, lips dark pink, eyes all blue,
"Pack up all my cares and woes, Here I go, swingin' low," as you
went inward, days, nights, "So make my bed and light the light,
I'll arrive late tonight…"

I couldn't see in, but could hear you, and all through the desert
night on your last ride you continued, passing cactus, passing
sage, your last instructions clear in my ear, "You're the one to be
sure I look right in the carriage, honey," all the way down Ramon
Road, past Date Palm Drive into Cathedral City, where the
cemetery lives, stop lights, go lights, with a wave of your white-
gloved hand, a Liza Minnelli smile, black cane tucked under your
armpit: "I said Blackbird, Oh, Blackbird, Bye, bye…"

On Metaphor

for Jane Hirshfield

> *Poetry is a Nation of People who know how to turn phrases on their heads.*
> —B.A. Van Sise, Photographer *Children of Grass*

No, Poetry is the moment
the falcon was placed on the poet's head

No, the moment she agreed
to be photographed like this

No, the moment the falcon's trainer arrived,
nervously articulated: "Well, he's not used to
being handled by anyone else."

No, the moment she then slid her hand
into the falconer's glove, the moment
the bird was raised up past her face

The moment the falcon's talons took their purchase
on her scarfed crown and the poet stood calmly, arms folded, the
hint of a smile as the hood was removed from the bird's eyes and
beak and what it meant, will mean in the years she has left in
stanza, in line, in phrase, in word, in syllable—giving as she has
her entire being to the grip of Poetry

To the Gun Dealers

There being some sixty-three thousand of you in America
more than two times the number of McDonalds and Starbucks

combined, I've thought long and hard about a suitable chorus
for this ode. I've decided on *Cry, the Beloved Country,* because

in the ancient Sixties my entire 10th-grade class once read it
chapter-by-chapter and at the end, the hero, Kumalo,
is left weeping for his son

executed for an act of gun violence. *Cry the Beloved Country*
because the actual number of guns in our sixty-three thousand
storefronts,

unprotected by any laws for how they are to be stored at any
given location, are that many wild lions living in our
communities…

Cry the Beloved Country because thefts do occur, you know, at
the time I was teaching 10th grade we had no lock-down drills,

and we were reading a novel about South Africa. *Cry the Beloved
Country,* because we have them now, lock-down-drills, special,

just for my grandchildren, and many, many Kumalos
are left, weeping, right here.

As Vinegar to the Teeth as Smoke to the Eyes

The Book of Proverbs, 23

Perhaps the Talmudist Rabbi Ulla is standing
in a Babylonian courtyard, having journeyed
from the holy land for this august meeting,
or perhaps Rabbi Hisda, who has just articulated
an interpretation on the *Mishnaic* commentary
of their teacher, Rabbi Yehuda, of blessed memory,
is standing in a courtyard in Israel, having journeyed hence
from Babylonia.

Important here: their reverence for the *Mishna*
and their zest to render it correctly for succeeding
generations, like mine. Rabbi Ulla wants to make clear to us the
vigor of his disagreement with the other's interpretation. *Not what
Rabbi Yehuda really said,* he thinks. Through generations of oral
memory and transcription he manages to call forth an ancient
riddle, a proverb, and he hisses:
"As vinegar to the teeth, as smoke to the eyes"
his words living on to be written down in the Talmud,
Ta'anit, Magillah 21, which I am studying
this very morning, the sky just clearing from the rain.

Hovering now in this room with me as he is,
Rabbi Hisda's teeth begin to ache again,
Rabbi Hisda's eyes begin to tear again, and all
because I am a lazy lady, not adept at the ancient
tongue, no longer capable of memorizing these texts, barely able
to make it to this study session on time, I have become the perfect
answer to the riddle of what it is that blurs the eyes of their vision,
like smoke, strips the teeth of their vigor, like vinegar:
a sluggard! Me.

A Marten, Two Girls, a Pit

A girl is trapped in a pit.
A young man rescues her.
They end up, for this is our
Talmud, embracing their ancient
story, pledging their love right there
with only the pit and a passing marten
as witnesses.

The rabbi who is telling this tale
raises his eyes to heaven, pauses,
then continues:

This young man forgets his vow, marries
another. They have two children.

The listeners, many young men themselves,
lean forward to catch the next words which
are falling
like rain from above
telling them at this point that if they
are faithful they will find that righteousness
will come down from heaven.

The rabbi continues staring straight into the empty
space before him. Both children, he says, die.
Tragically. One by falling into a pit, the other bitten
by a marten.

I think the young men listening are sweating
under their garments. Then, the rabbi actually
says, right in the middle of our Talmud,
that these unusual deaths made the young
man realize his error and he returned to the
first woman!

I am destroyed. I, the mother of the children,
I, bereft of blessings, mortified, alone. "What
was she doing in the pit in the first place?"I scream
into the closed vault of the heavens above me,
"And, who is left to protect me, in *this* pit
when the marten returns for *me* as well?"

The Fishpond and Rabbi Ilfi

for Sarah Dina, born in November

Once in your country long ago, Sarah Dina, there was a great drought. Everyone prayed and prayed. They even fasted, but no rain came. One morning Rabbi Ilfi was asked to lead the service. He recited: "He who makes the wind blow," and lo and behold, the wind blew! Then he said, "He who makes the rain fall." And lo and behold, the rain fell!

"Oh, Rabbi Ilfi" they exclaimed joyfully, "What are your good deeds that merit this answer to our prayers?"

"I am," said Rabbi Ilfi, "a teacher of small children, rich and poor, but if any child cannot pay, he learns with me. Also, if any child struggles to learn, I say, 'Come child, look.' And I sit with him at my fishpond to watch my fish swim over sky-blue tiles spackled with green reeds. Any child who looks into it can see small souls with fins and tails swish in their watery heaven until his own soul is at ease and can swim then, can glide effortlessly across the lettered parchment, following my slowly moving finger."

May your little eyes, that first opened in the light of Jerusalem today, always swim in ponds of pleasantness, and may the letters set before them dance with joy.

11/12/20

In Transit, The Galapagos

Past our sleeping forms, the blue-silk pajama-clad you,
the minty cotton-gowned me, drift the ashes Guayaquilanos
have produced in their wild burnings for this New Year—
effigies of the whole year's evils they've made, large with terrible
grins, or poor decapitated remnants, foreshortened, standing or
lying ghastly at the curbs, as the Guayas River carries tufts of
living grasses toward the gulf, the sea…

We sleep at such a large window, our last night spent huddled
together before the unknown separates us once more, me to the
north, you to the south as this Rio huge with Ecuador and its dark
pushes tufts of living grasses toward the gulf, the sea, spore of
what will feed turtle, iguana, blue-footed booby, penguin, sea
lion, seed of what will emerge to climb its way onto the black
volcanic isles uplifted, out-spewed, we two outcroppings of an old
desire resting now as the terrible past moves past us each second,
water-borne, you saying what you always say after we've torn
into each other, *It's in the past, love,* as the sea turtles turn and
mate in the deep, as the land turtles mount, are mounted in the
highland grass, then rip off sweet mouthfuls of it, the eternal
grass, which floats toward them in the long night to hover and
pass above them in the morning's beaming turquoise light, above
which the black frigates will soar again, their long, forked tails
cutting all our tomorrows into this one last today.

1/1/20

VI. I Dream of Snow—2020

The Well

for Ari Chicheportiche
August 2020

Your big blue right eye
had a small star in it
when you face-timed me
for the first time, my little
great-grandson, as if you had
just been taken from a crystal
blue lake in your white pajamas
with blue cranes and elephants
cavorting across them

And that lake had a deep place
where the star came from.

"Why not the sky?" you will ask
when you get older

Hmm. I like to think that I was the sky
and the star came from me, fell into
the lake and emerged in the well of your eye!

"You were the sky?" you will ask
when you get older

Hmm. I like to think I was that blue,
that full of limitless love, little great-grandson,
the first time I saw you…

On the Death of John Prine

It's been years since the woman I've become
has heard you sing, but I'm sitting in a house
of wood among oak trees remembering that voice
of yours as it once carved deep streams among
the rocks we traversed, backpacks on our shoulders
our three kids upfront or trailing behind, and the small
Sierra towns we'd driven through into the California
backcountry, dog wagging her tail in someone's
face, or on our yearly trek to the Trinity River, always
in the presence of your gravelly tones, keen eye, perfect
listening ear, riotous humor, a bowl of oatmeal staring
you down, you'd twang or you'd tell us about losing
Davy in the Korean War, O, *Hello in There,* John Prine,
I can't eat a peach without the words of your *Spanish
Pipedream* coming in through my teeth with the taste,
the juice, and those instructions of yours "Blow up your TV"
rocked my mind today when I heard you'd gone down
into our national outrage, our huge Covid-19 annals where
the truest American voice I've ever heard had just
expired…

4/8/20

For Judy in Manhattan

> *But how alien, alas, are the streets of the city of grief;*
> *where in the false silence formed in continual uproar,*
> *the figure cast from the mold of Emptiness stoutly*
> *swaggers*
> —Rilke, *The Tenth Elegy*
> translated by Stephen Mitchell

A girl named J washing the floors of her apartment in Manhattan vacuuming the carpets, dusting the shelves surrounded by canvases of color said to me, "He's an alien. That's why/ He doesn't get sick and die," not realizing it rhymed, as when reading *Sonnets to Orpheus* so busy with the English I forget to glance across at the German…

J, watching the virus multiply by subtraction down there in the streets Central Park now too crowded for those early morning walks of hers until her last one, past the large tents set up in waiting. J now walking the verticals, up and down instead of out and out, up and down the stairwells pausing now and again for breath, her shadow bent over the next step, the next…

A girl named J washing the floors of her apartment in Manhattan vacuuming the carpets, dusting the shelves surrounded by canvases of color thinking, "But how alien, alas, are the streets of the city of grief," not knowing it rhymed with thief, with chief, with fief, or maybe she did as she walked the verticals, step-by-step-by step, and the bodies piled

high into the freezer trucks; and the mass grave trenches were dug by prisoners freed from the local penitentiary to do this, and the bodies unclaimed were sunk in, as the girl named J washed the floors of her apartment in Manhattan, vacuumed the carpets, dusted the shelves surrounded by canvases of color as that figure, cast from the mold of Emptiness stoutly swaggered…

4/13/20

For Susie in Minneapolis

I saw America flaming
in her covid mask struggling to break free
of all the racist pain that marks her bankrupt
passage through pandemic and the ruined generations of her
multi-colored love

She who once broke free of one tyrant
to land herself under another

I saw America flaming
in her covid mask struggling to break free
of old forms, of hatred's two best friends,
violence and decay

I saw police lined up in her cities
suddenly taking a knee
opposite the brave and kneeling protesters

knee to cement
the only gesture
beginning to redeem
the knee that pressed so hard
upon George Floyd whose life
the moment it flew from him became
this torch to set America
marching through her cities
gathering in her squares flaming
in her covid mask struggling to break free

6/1/20

On Seeing the Comet Noewise

Traipsing up a pot-holed hill in the dark after
three nights of not seeing you—bingo! There
you were, just over a notch in the horizon spraying
the darkening sky with your silver tail, your nose
pointed down toward us here on Earth. When next
you pass, 7,000 years hence, will there be human
life left to observe you? We aren't doing so well:
today 511,600 of us have died in a global pandemic.
just a drop, I know, in that bucket named the Big
Dipper hanging over you tonight, once seen by ancient
astronomers as a big bier instead, the stars on its handle
as mourners.

May the silent beauty of your icy spray blowing in solar winds
continue to exist in memory of those who have left, are leaving us
as you arched above us in the long night that is time and space
beyond our comprehension.

7/21/20

Man Dreaming

> "I was asleep, but my heart was awake."
> —Song of Songs 5:2

Fully clothed
pillowed head facing
a TV talk show
Calle Libertad sounding
at the window he drowses
I touch his arm, say,
"Are you asleep?"
"—No! No, it's ok!"
and then we are walking
toward the Alexander Bridge, no less,
"one of the most beautiful river-crossings
in the world," heart of Paris, sumptuous
with lions, cherubs, nymphs, cupids, water spirits,
fish, seashells, sea monsters—when this man dreams, he dreams
big. Turns to me "We are not far
from Shakespeare and Company, we could go there…"

"And then you woke up? You were so lucky,"
I say, meaning so lucky to have dreamt we were
in Paris together. "Lucky?" He laughs. "Yes, every
day we wake up still here we are lucky! We can go to the
refrigerator, take a shower! Lucky!"
Just like that he leaves me in Paris…

8/5/20
15 Av, Hebrew calendar, Day of Love

I Dream of Snow

Minnesota baby rolled up in blankets carried
out into biting January air. Perhaps it was
snowing the day I first journeyed forth into
the human stream, and perhaps my first ride home
in a car my mother whispered something to me or my
young father leaned over to see if I were ok, does

that explain my hunger for snow, those landscapes
of miraculous coverings and pokings-out, the airy
wisp of flakes thudding against my cheek? Does
that explain the alternate universe of the ice skating
rink, the spins and dives of wet blades shining, scraping
the ice in bold figures, a language of body writing thrilling
me to the core, the crunch of white underfoot, the drip
of the translucent edging our eaves and the world-blinding
mystery of blizzards that stop—everything?

This year one of our presidential candidates stood in it,
the snow, and allowed it to net and re-net her brown hair
without covering it, without a hat to declare, yes, she was
in that race to take back our nation. My eyes were wet as I
watched on TV. Yes, I do want the nation restored, yes, I did like
what she said, but it was the flakes coming down on her head
arriving from another world, transforming all who stood there
with her that I ultimately voted for.

12/31/20

About the Author

Fairfax, California poet, memoir practitioner, and literary translator Doreen Stock recently launched *Bye Bye Blackbird,* a collection of poems about her mother's last days (Poetry Box, 2021). Other works include: *Your Excellency, Free Will,* poems translated with Marcelo Holot from the Spanish of Amparo Casasbellas Alconada (Prosa Amerian Editores, 2021); *Tango Man,* a collection of love poems (Finishing Line Press, 2020); *My Name is Y,* an anti-nuclear memoir (Norfolk Press, 2019); *Three Tales from the Archives of Love,* a work of historical fiction (Norfolk Press, 2018); *Talking with Marcelo,* a book-length interview of Argentine Journalist Marcelo Holot (Mine Gallery Editions, 2017); *In Place of Me,* poems edited and introduced by Jack Hirschman (Mine Gallery Editions, 2015); *The Politics of Splendor,* poems and translations (Alcatraz Editions, Santa Cruz, 1984). An interview and reading of Doreen's poetry can be viewed online at Marin Poet's Live! She is a founding member of The Marin Poetry Center. For more information: doreenstock.com.

www.ingramcontent.com/pod-product-compliance
Lightning Source LLC
Chambersburg PA
CBHW032237080426
42735CB00008B/889

TRANSIENCE

ACT THREE

Leaving base camp
humping pyre stick bundles
under sacred mountain vows of
noble silence, no lamentation, not knowing,
I ascend my bespoke Narayama
seeking the invisible house builder,
ice spikes grip avoiding attachment avalanches
sweeping me into crevasses of panicked regrets
of which, as Francis Albert sang,
I've had a few.

Questions arise.
Should I have stayed or gone?
What really mattered most?
Did I love well enough?
Was it worth it?
Consigliere doubt whispers
turn right, turn left, no, go straight,
straining to hear my internal GPS
rear vision wisdom laser lights
hindsight's elusive genius.

Time left is measured in dog years
tricked by each turning
seemingly faster than the last,
cheated rage ravages once
straight spines osteoporosis-bent,
grey-lobed memories vacuumed
dancing on Covid cruises,
no fools like old fools,
Titanic bucket lists ticked
not waving, drowning.

LOST IN TRANSIT

Carousel python
snakes backstage
shedding baggage,
boarding call
heralds anonymity,
who am I?
Excess baggage
lost in transit,
fasten seatbelts,
arm doors,
prepare for take-off.

AS I PASSES BY

Pleasure, pain
love, loneliness,
those old familiar things.
Weren't you someone once?
Gripping nostalgia's balcony
watching strolling memories
as if they were
real as the balustrade,
perception's fingers
point at the moon,
as I passes by.

FULLNESS OF TIME

Schoolyard shout,
nicked bat – howzat!
Dandelion snow floats
in summer haze.

Make a wish,
if feathery parachutes
blow away at once
dreams will come true.

Morning's open florets
wilt in afternoon sun,
snapping lockers trap
stale boy smells.

MEMENTO MORI

Time's flyover
scans for what
was, before
fading memory
hid everything.

The beat your heart skips
disrupts the sinus rhythm
of vascular irrigation,
in the gap
memento mori.

Trees you climbed
not so tall now,
a girl you once kissed
serves designer coffee
in the old lawnmower shop.

LAST NIGHT

We sat up until midnight
singing familiar songs, telling stories
as your breath rattled
around the darkened room.

Hoping in these last moments
you remember your lived merit,
letting go in love
under the night lamp glow.

Thinking, last mind moment,
next mind moment,
don't die in fear,
know how much we love you.

We kissed your shrunken cheeks,
assuring you of
our watchful
embracing presence.

Nuns fingered the kingdom keys
nurses turned you
modulating the palliative flow,
hail, Holy Mother of Morphine.

You opened your eyes
offering two small puffs of breath,
death's finality witnessed,
you're here, you're not.

Your spirit shell
reverently washed and shaved
agape jaw supported
against death's stiffening chill.

Heaven, hell, reincarnation,
all blank cheques
beside the patiently waiting
velvet burgundy body bag.

Departure's arrival sensed
Mum signals the young funeral attendant
entrusting him with your bandstand tuxedo
for the final gig.

COMING AND GOING

Death leaves
no pleasure unperturbed
vaporising past glories
vainly hailing Caesar
against downward thumbs.

Plea bargaining
bedside vigils
stalked by death
when grief leaves
the room to urinate.

In the existential share house
birth rends the veil
across the light,
death draws the blind
coming and going as it pleases.

NO REGRETS

Your loyal blonde Pacific semi-acoustic
leans against the pine coffin
in the packed church.

Re-tuned every Sunday before you
accompany Mum on the hymnal organ
her curtain call echoing from downstairs.

Shutting your guitar case
you remonstrate against her hurry-up,
replying, 'it's only a few minutes away.'

This time you're there before everyone.
Behind your mortal encasement
robed priests bustle at the flower-strewn altar.

Kaleidoscopic light rays stream
through stained glass church windows,
your leadlighting converted for Jesus.

Besuited ageing mates in Sunday best
thumb the photocopied funeral book,
recalling another clansman lost.

The towns's fading generation
testimony to your rhetorical homage,
'Where would you find better people?'

They watch me, listening intently
as I eulogise you radiating joy
jamming in guitar heaven.

*

Mornings along the Great Ocean Road
searching for the perfect wave,
your crutches discarded at the water's edge.

You're first in hopping on one leg
whooping as you ride the crest of the wave,
your disability disregarded.

Later as a fierce Paralympian bowler
you discover your tribe,
a proud mentor to its indomitable spirit.

In a city jazz club, seemingly 20 years younger,
you track complex improvisation,
shouting 'yeah man' in time with the beat.

*

As Alzheimer's numbing vines slowly spread
carers chauffeur you on weekly cafe tastings
searching for the best apple crumble.

Anticipating your daily meal on wheels
you call from the front window, 'hey Bet, lunch's here',
eagerly lifting the plastic lids for favourites.

'I don't know what I'd do without you,'
Mum tenderly affirms your preciousness,
'but you don't have to, I'm still here', you cheerfully reply.

'Do you ever think about death?' I once ask.
Dissolving my earnestness you quip,
'not while I'm still alive'.

*

At your funeral, fearful of her frailty,
I stay close to Mum whispering 'how you doing?'
'Better than I should be' she says, relieved at her surprise.

'Perhaps it's because I have no regrets', she observes,
an epiphanic equation, having left nothing undone,
no rueful wishing to be had.

As strong men lower you into the fresh grave
rosemary twigs nourishing death land softly
among earthen reminders of our cyclical return.

As a silent formal rite
at military attention
my brother salutes his last farewell.

*

Later at the wake, the Catholic Ladies Guild
unveils a countrywomen's spread
of sucrose-elevated conviviality.

Known family and friends I've never met
step inside my blurred personal space
to testify to your kind heart.

People care about you here,
verifying your 'village tragic' claims
of it being 'the best place on earth'.

Your Italian bowling partner swears
you always brought him luck,
that competitive streak never giving up.

The elocution teacher sternly compliments
my eulogy's content and enunciation,
a tradesman's work-worn hand grips mine.

'That's the man I remember', he assures me,
just as you told Mum before slipping away,
'everything's working out'.

BIRTHDAY

Another year older,
mortality's breath on my neck
time's vulture on my shoulder,
the reflection in the mirror
seems like someone I once knew.

All time is grace to proceed apace
to say what's unsaid, do what's undone,
defuse landmines undetected,
bow to everyone respected,
Vote 1 Wisdom, still unelected.

Media bogans shout botox slogans.
60 is the new 40
grey is the new black,
read all about how
your hair will grow back.

This is no sad song
each New Year's resolution vows
to let go, to love anew, to embrace
friends on the path, who can still laugh
at the absurdity of clinging to the raft.

When you're moved
by gratitude
for the time granted,
forgiving them against whom you've ranted
seeking same of those you've supplanted.

No time for enemies, just time for friends,
no time for fighting, time for amends,
time to take time, time to have tea,
time to sit still, time to be free,
time moves faster when you're getting on.

Time to make sense of what's to be done,
no time like the present,
the future is never here,
this time's the last,
time's lost in the past.

GONE

Every pleasure desired
every treasure admired
every deal transpired
every date expired.

Every storm abated
every enemy hated
every celebrity feted
every idea debated.

Every chasm leapt
every floor swept
every lover wept
every secret kept.

Every fear fed
every rumour spread
every palm read
every tear shed.

Every doubt resolved
every sin absolved
every stage evolved
every marriage dissolved.

Every accolade earned
every judgment discerned
every new leaf turned
every book burned.

Every fact known
every seed sown
every chance blown
every coop flown.

THE SPACE BETWEEN

in

the

space

between

Roistering rapids churn
shuddering salmon seek
spawning's fateful turn.

the

space

in

between

Tremulous tongue tips
trigger electric beats
of passionate palpitations.

in

between

the

space

Deliberately deeper breaths
becalm fears betwixt
this moment and the next.

between

the

space

in

Composed imagined boundaries
of white and black notes,
all music exists.

the

in

between

space

Beneath shadow's guile
deception's subterranean subversion
hides schadenfreude's smile.

in

space

between

the

Architect's blueprint instruction
projecting future ruins
of desire's construction.

NEGATION QUARTET

No

No standing
no stopping
no credit
no shopping

no resemblance
no relation
no pain
no sedation

no preservatives
no flavours
no promises
no favours

no worries
no sweat
no problem
no threat

no time
no space
no future
no place

no man
no fear
no woman
no tear

no guts
no glory
no sex
no story

no cheating
no lying
no killing
no dying

no mercy
no hope
no vision
no dope

no black
no white
no left
no right

no self
no view
no me
no you

Not

Not a moment
not a chance
not a dream
not a trance

not a tool
not a knife
not a fool
not a wife

not a picnic
not a lark
not a walk
not a park

not a man
not a fixture
not a woman
not a mixture

not a robot
not a slave
not a rehearsal
not a grave

not a messiah
not a tout
not a question
not a doubt

not a giver
not a taker
not a mover
not a shaker

not a theory
not a fact
not a believer
not a tract

not a sentence
not a crime
not a couplet
not a rhyme

not a thought
not a reason
not a bird
not a season

not a contest
not a race
not a clue
not a trace

No one

No one remembered
no one explained
no one thought
no one complained

no one answered
no one cried
no one laughed
no one died

no one came
no one went
no one stayed
no one sent

no one pushed
no one shoved
no one felt
no one loved

no one lied
no one thought
no one decried
no one caught

no one home
no one spared
no one here
no one cared

no one sinned
no one blamed
no one better
no one named

no one forgotten
no one denied
no one asked
no one replied

no one gained
no one trusted
no one charged
no one busted

no one excluded
no one believed
no one suffered
no one conceived

no one saw
no one broke
no one heard
no one spoke

Nothing

Nothing ventured
nothing saved
nothing lost
nothing craved

nothing found
nothing recovered
nothing taken
nothing discovered

nothing happened
nothing bidden
nothing gleaned
nothing hidden

nothing seen
nothing clear
nothing heard
nothing here

nothing said
nothing bleeped
nothing sown
nothing reaped

nothing kept
nothing sent
nothing left
nothing spent

nothing recorded
nothing appeared
nothing moved
nothing feared

nothing lasts
nothing brewing
nothing matters
nothing doing

nothing broken
nothing owned
nothing borrowed
nothing loaned

nothing given
nothing earned
nothing stolen
nothing returned

nothing happened
nothing exposed
nothing existed
nothing composed

TIME AND PLACE

SORRY

Kevin's Sorry was symbolic,
a white bread cucumber sandwich Sorry
to make our black history go down easier
burying a genocide
excising the thousands
of Indigenous Australians murdered
under policies of extermination,
Kevin was Sorry we weren't Sorry earlier
but truth was that earlier
we weren't even Sorry,
it was before our time,
and although we're really Sorry
for what happened then
it wasn't actually us that did it,
Sorry about that,
being Sorry doesn't mean we owe you,
it's time to move on, Sorry,
you can't make us feel more Sorry
we talked about that earlier, Sorry,
look, we've said Sorry, haven't we?
you're starting to make us feel Sorry
we even mentioned it,
just get over it, okay?
Sorry.

ALL YOUR CHRISTMASES

Imagine all your Christmases have come at once
invading like marine corps grunts
Christ is born only to disappear
like ice baths full of Christmas cheer
waiting for the rellos to
deck the halls with total recall
of every overstuffed lunch.

Imagine all your Christmases have come at once
Dad's out back teaching torpedo punts,
the nod to the Messiah is only token
like the dope your sister's smoking
children's toys already broken
three wise men, a weeping turkey hen
neon nativity flashing now and then.

Imagine all your Christmases have come at once
all the best take a rest
everyone's over here and over blown
sacred presents laid before the chosen one
Aunty June's not talking to anyone
brother Ken can't make it
calls reverse charges.

Imagine all your Christmases have come at once
with all their Santa-slaying family stunts
tension rising with the temperature
Mum sits on the collective fears
beach balls exploding in the sun
Trevor's downed 20 beers
Grandma's praying we're having fun.

Imagine all your Christmases have come at once,
just like *The Scream* a la Edvard Munch
dreaming of a white Christmas
even though it's burned black
smoke alarms ring in decorated McMansions
Santa's stuck in the chimney
trapped by his sack.

BYRON SHADOWS

First light strikes rock flint
igniting sparks across volcanic ranges
lighting fuses of conical explosions
steaming seas solidify cascading lava
whale spumes spray cooling mist
beneath arching rainbow thunderclouds
machine gun Koels signal symphonic sunrise
of feathered waking arias.

Mammal spirits guard secret slaughterhouses
soothing tear-soaked suffering aeons
morning sun rays radiate
illuminating shadows, stirring unconscious sleepers
alpha dolphins leap crystal waves
painted indigene custodians dance dreamings
reflected against frozen forest firelight
falling writhing under bullet hail.

Escapee white tortured souls
kill blacks, whales, cows, then themselves
sad women watch fearfully loathing
womb children inherit hate holocaust
overloaded blood boats dispatch groaning
spoils, milky forest, black blubber
respectable money mows fat land
balding wild hills, silencing oceans.

Newly discovered dreamers magnetically drawn
chant tantra, love-sexy mantras
floating babies sprout angel wings
flooding the promised land with blessed beings
backpacker Bedouins beckon international caravanserai
greedily disgorging at tourist pilgrim mecca
Rasta vibrations wobble towards Jah headland
pulsating with Instagram memories.

Toothless grey dreadlocked men drive
fierce, pierced, feral Kombis
naked sadhus surf inflatable tridents
glass-eyed fundamentalists stone sinners
fatherless children evacuate family landfill
stonewashed red-rimmed hero dads
slouch angrily demanding feminine affections
fire-twirlers spin endless, faithful, flame sticks.

THIS IS NOT INDIA

'This is not India,'
cries the blue-eyed English yogi,
spitting blood red betel
as he re-lights his next beedi
with a splintering, spluttering match.

Is it the painted elephant in downtown Delhi traffic,
shading a blind beggar, his eyes seemingly pecked out by crows,
or the lopsided gypsy, one foot in the gutter,
dragging a lumbering sloth bear?

'This is not India,'
scowls the weathered,
worldly-wise German backpacker,
sipping a street corner chai
from a small, chipped, opaque glass.

Is it the chanting, ash-smeared mendicant,
collecting his urine in a bottle through a plastic tube from his penis
as he begs from door to door, beneath billowing silk saris
and monkeys leaping across rooftops?

'This is not India,'
sniffs the ageing French hippie,
a speck of rice stuck on her nose ruby
as she stabs her ring-covered fingers
into a 30-rupee thali.

Is it the beflowered schoolgirls,
piled high in rickshaws, giggling innocently and shouting,
'Hi, hello, what's your name?'
before collapsing with laughter at their brazen dare?

'This is not India,'
snorts the pneumatic,
Lycra-shorted American cyclist,
charging through crowds in ski glasses
on his fold-up, 36-speed mountain bike.

Is it the interwoven, permanent cacophony
of jangling bike bells and clamouring klaxons
or the bull roar of lurching trucks and buses,
bearing down like rampaging drunken elephants?

THIS IS INDIA

'This is India!'
the holy man intones
as a billion sacred mantras
chant via cell phone ring tones,
atop an overloaded cart
matchstick men whip patient bullocks,
computer screensavers reveal
Sita and Rama in Hanuman's heart.

'This is India!'
sacred cows ruminate nonchalantly
in the onslaught of masala traffic,
mangy dogs doze mid-road
taxi drivers must be telepathic,
surrendering to larger vehicular species
avoiding road rage ragas
on the highway of the faeces.

'This is India!'
barks the moustachioed superintendent
the law is straight
until you bend it,
his cane lathi stick pointing
to an imaginary queue
pockets stuffed with rupees
as vituperative VIPs negotiate a better view.

'This is India!'
headstrong women shout, a nation's load
balanced deftly on their crowns,
brilliant, rainbow-hued saris
dazzle the shadows of their frowns,
bent-double, ancient girl mothers
carry rented babies in their arms
synchronistically gesturing with upturned palms.

'This is India!'
'Out of stock madam,
come back day after tomorrow',
the pukka shopkeeper enunciates
post-colonially rounding his vowels
deflating bloated foreign tourists
seeking soft toilet paper
for their exploding bowels.

'This is India!'
the suffering clerk explains with grace
the duty officer is 'out of station,
gone to his native place',
handing me a flimsy form
my visit noted on a chit, he demands
'purpose of your visit, father's name
all signed in triplicate.'

'This is India!'
the exuberant entrepreneur enthuses
'Everyone's a winner now, nobody loses',
the tiger's stripes are globalised
a new call centre caste system revitalised
by gated sweatshops glistening in the sun,
where weary www wage slaves
drop out one by one.

'This is India!'
whispers the wizened untouchable
with a knowing wobble of his head,
the mighty Dalit serpent is waking
equality's slumber from its bed,
a sleeping giant marshals the oppressed underground
filling Vishnu's victory conch
with freedom's roaring sound.

MILES

The segregated states
of racist America
relegated derided brilliance
to the back of the bus,
skull-cracking batons
pummelled its tonal palette,
black jazz lived underground
or took the Paris option
where the artist mattered.

Your body immobile
forming a question mark
fearless eyes returning anger,
only the dangerous
don't bow and scrape,
when critics ask
where the music's going
a voice whispering over gravel
declares this present address.

Clarion trumpet seizes
the notes you want
that no one else gets
not an entertainer
but a sound,
every signature album
turning form on its head,
the only way to understand
you is to be you.

That round modal sound,
not too much tremolo
or too much bass
in the right place
soothing a million nights
birthing the cool
manipulating space,
muted gestures of power
creating a new orality.

Prince of Darkness
play it first and tell them afterwards
you have to play a long time
to be able to play like yourself,
the thing to judge is
does a man have ideas,
you're not going to play the blues anymore
let white folks play the blues
they got 'em, so they can keep 'em.

The Dark Magus does not
fear mistakes, there are none,
don't play what's there
play what's not
revolution follows the music,
don't call him a legend
that's an old man with a cane
known for what he used to do.
You're still doing it.

THE RETREAT

Arriving

Ghosts of the past register years later
Ron leans on his walking stick with a marionette tilt
shadowed by Sarah who died from anaphylaxis
when the ambulance failed to arrive in time.

With resolute diligence
young Tom checks my application form
last time I saw him he was seven years old
dancing in my lounge room.

Now he works in IT
studying philosophy online
I muse that love of wisdom
is due for a comeback any time now.

Storeroom jester Phil wears an 'ask me' button,
years ago on a soul black night
he lay drunk on a railway line
waking to discover the train was cancelled.

I request two single sheets,
three blankets and a firm flat pillow,
laughing, he gifts me a new, pink hot water bottle
reminding me 'it's bloody freezing in the mornings.'

Beginning

Wind-whipped eucalyptus pom poms
form a rousing cheer squad
of rustling leaf brushed snares,
crash-riding tin roof cymbals.

Under the spreading night ink
thrashing branches exfoliate
tree trunks shaken avian-free,
sans screech, crow-craw repartee.

Where do the birds go?
Grounded in the undergrowth
feather-huddled humming
unsung sky songs between sorties.

Under an ascetic single lightbulb
I shave my head as a preventive fire break
against Buddha's exhortation
to practise as if my hair was aflame.

Thick mud straw bale walls
embrace blue blanket-wrapped students
mispronouncing monastic vows,
hope triumphing over linguistic transgressions.

In the pregnant pre-dawn
row upon row upon row of
rowers in the same boat
rearrange their neural deck chairs.

Iceberg starboard, vessel taking water,
separated from everything owned
personal baggage sinks like leaden flab,
as if there's nothing left to grab.

A nodding field of sentinel minds,
drowsy merit makers and procrastinators,
attempt to prevent flickering memories
turning into ruminative narratives.

Backs against the wall
facing familiar foes
transient semaphore of the matador's cape
distracts their clawing, steaming charge.

Silently musing all compounded things
continually changing, unmanageable,
eventually falling apart,
but hopefully not just yet.

Row, row, row your boat
entering the stream,
verily, verily, verily, verily,
life is but a dream.

Noticing

Notice recollected remains of life
recorded in skin, muscle, bone,
buried thoughts, feelings, valence
revealed in archaeo-conscious dig.

Notice nostril breath minutiae,
length, temperature, pauses,
activating mental voicemail,
'no one's in right now.'

Notice collective breakfast anxiety
anticipating arising of the toast,
absorbed by awe-inspiring Vegemite label
revealing salt as second highest ingredient.

Notice teacher intoning 'changing, changing',
as mind shouts 'impermanent'
at resolute knee agony,
saved by the lunch gong.

Notice entitlement arising seeing
sweets sign saying 'take one only',
next day turning to righteousness
when it reads 'take two only.'

Notice mute post-lunch bushwalkers avoiding contact,
deftly boot scooting on narrow tracks
while trembling pristine raindrops
merge in surrender on autumnal twigs.

Notice fantasy cruising calm seas
of life with the cute, composed woman
at the end of the third row,
I think her name's Louise.

Notice stomach gripping recognising
visceral vacuum of absent biological father,
discovering suffering's mutuality hearing
a sobbing meditator at the back of the hall.

Notice reflected emotions
in the mirror of attention
suddenly passing on my blind side
much, much, closer than previously apparent.

Burning

In a single, solitary cell, some might call it hell,
I'm taking the cure,
listening to my personal black box
replaying in hi-fi sense-surround.

Its transcript records back teeth lies
always thinking I'm right,
hoping the emergency life drill
will get me through the night.

Once a crutch,
old ally anger becomes an accuser
evidence of everything done and said
imploding shrapnel in my head.

Reliving every betrayal takes its toll
slumped sweat-soaked, suddenly unwell,
did I really just pulp an imagined enemy
against the pagoda walls?

Riding emotion's elevator
down to anger's basement of grief
finds imprisoned plea bargainer
shouting 'get me out of here.'

I'm the reaper and the sower
victim and abuser, dealer and user,
not a postcode without a map,
it's time to take the rap.

No original sin to correct
whichever class I select
personal baggage accompanies me
courtesy of cause and effect.

En route retreat, my lover texted we're no more
now she's here in every aching pore,
I beg Buddha for an answer,
inner voice replies, 'just let go.'

Releasing

Watchtower's swooping beam
highlights previously impenetrable porosity
intermittent, wavering, loosening
glue stick of addiction.

Magnet of attended sensations
stalls moist, rough pink tongues
of wolves slavering by my side
before they turn heel.

Things known or unknown
don't seem to matter anymore,
daydreaming in warm deep grass
watching soft thought pillows drift past.

Waking voice shakes dealt hand
cleaning the bowl of emptiness
with the cloth of tenderness,
cherishing everyone and everything.

Returning

Does unbounded friendliness
penetrate concrete walls?
Unconditional love melts bodies into the floor
flooding all species two legs and more.

Time to greet fellow travellers
sharing healing balm
on wounds from arrows
slung before the calm.

Veteran retreaters hold sway,
a novice stripper disrobes their sins
I spy Louise kissing the female manager
behind the recycling bins.

Heading home, mountain winding down,
suburban still life passes by,
ants in honey, buzzing flies on meat,
hungry ghosts queueing without a seat.

Masked niceties discarded
morning wears a permanent frown
kindness gets taken down,
suck it up, cop it sweet.

Stuck on a six-lane bridge
one open hearted empathic
smiles at red light pauses
of bumper-to-bumper traffic.

Exchanging themselves for
cold coffee, lurking redundancy,
cancer diagnosis, broken love
ingesting peak hour frustration.

Breathing in toxic fuming shadow
breathing out, unlimited friendly
24/7 roadside assistance
dissolving gridlocked separation.

Window wound down
fear blown away,
fresh morning breeze
extinguishes fired strife.

Quenching thirst
soothing heart
calming mind
cooling life.

THE MONTHS

Once upon a time
in ancient Mesopotamia
the moon's orbit
became a lunation,
dividing the lunar cycle
into 12 monthly mansions.

30 (odd) days
720 hours
43,200 minutes
2,592,000 seconds.

Ebbing tides,
flowing blood,
Sun, moon tango.
Life's diurnal churning
measured on calendars.

January

New Year's resolutions
melt like ice cream
in the midday sun,
languid beached bodies
becalmed by the nasal
drone of cricket commentary
turn bright red
under dangerous skies,
the twin face of Janus
looking forward, looking back,
landscape burning bushfire black,
wailing sirens clear the water.
Shark attack!

February

Late summer furnace
- hottest on record -
inheriting the planetary grill,
sweating children glower
on expectation's treadmill,
workers accelerating apace
yearn for a gentler human face
as holiday memories
melt amid traffic jams,
in a lonely paddock
of swollen dying stock,
a broken farmer
fingers his last bullet.

March

Striding towards the Ides
Mars' wrathful grindstone
hones eager noses,
electronic wallpaper declares
all life is football!
Warring suburban tribes
cheer leather trajectories
across perfect skies,
cosmetically modified blondes
dance for beer and pies,
penitent peacemakers fast
observing Lenten rituals,
preparing for new beginnings
with an eye on the heavenly goal.

April

Hot cross preachers
project PowerPoint shrouds,
holy fools work the crowds
rendering unto Instagram
all that is Google,
Easter Bunny believers
hop towards Jerusalem
chanting, 'love the stranger
for you were once strangers in Egypt',
65 million homeless humans
drift on indifference,
as sugar-craving children furiously
hunt chocolate treasure.

May

On Buddha's full moon
of birth, awakening and passing,
winter's steel glints
in the fading light
of yellowing leaves
surrendering to gravity.
Soup returns from retreat!
Liberated naphthalene woollens
somersault in rejoicing dryers,
cyclists' wet noses
sniff the first wisps
of burning fires on
the cool ride home.

June

Short-changed, night's curtain
falls without warning on
another snap frozen relationship,
winter radio cries a river
of suddenly profound break-up songs,
hearts shrivel like salted fish,
she loves me,
she loves me not,
she loves me,
but she can't live with me,
her consolation of
'still being friends'
drives a nail
through my shoe.

July

Viral respiration sniffs
in united discontent
at our privileged white entitlement,
another refugee boat sinks
as the asylum blows its nose
on selfish land legalism,
trumpeting compassion's last post
for protracted detained days
and longer lonely nights,
hanging out at airports
in barren expectation,
while my mind stalks
happy holiday destinations.
We are all boat people.

August

The cruellest month,
avocado interiors secretly darken,
a shadow cast by
a lover on a pedestal,
prescient buds proffer hope
of winter's loosening grip,
31 more gritted days
friends basking in Bali,
post-modernising in Berlin,
pilgriming on the Camino,
a Parisian postcard arrives,
sealed with a lipstick kiss.

September

Explosions of pink blossom
detonate love's entombment,
thawing frozen Eros,
slow cooked from the inside
now wrapped in warmer air
Greenland's ice sheets melt
Manhattan-sized glaciers,
mining billionaires buy
good carbon news forever,
Spring's light dances on high beam,
spotlighting unswaddled bodies
darting through green shoots
in happy dog parks.

October

Time beckons towards
the year's end,
demanding clock watchers
toe the bottom line.
What's been achieved
despite all that's been said?
Prostrated before market forces,
politicians practise 'free' trade voodoo,
factory gates close
like coffin lids
on the globalised dead,
a train is coming down the track,
who will leave on it?
She's never coming back.

November

The sombreness
of the indelible 11,
9/11 Berlin Wall falls to freedom
11/11 'The War to End All Wars'
and, lest we forget,
7/11, open 24/7.
Daylight saving stretches time
illuminating al fresco intimacies
of love's possibility again,
hope's sputtering neon highlights
breathlessly sucked in stomachs
emerging from hibernation,
shuddering against the transparency
of last year's swimmers.

December

Christmas cash registers jingle,
can baby Jesus still turn a profit?
Frenzied shoppers ring
consumption's sacred bells,
death-defying punters
gaze at life's sushi train of
fallen friends,
fragility survived,
stuff acquired.
Where did the year go?
What's it all about?
Everyone wants to live forever,
but no one wants to
when they get there.
Unable to live in doubt
we make up the best story possible.

LOVE TIDES

IMAGINARY LOVE

Imaginary love
launches a million crooners
singing Blue Moon
out of tune.

Helpless honeymooners
bedtime spooners
crying a river
only monsoon tears deliver.

In physically distant nights
lovers recite invisible poems
of bending willows
on fantasy pillows.

He'll change for her
she'll stay the same
to the letter
tick box for better.

Hearing sirens singing
sailors steer ships blinded
by desire's projections
onto rocks of mermaid reflections.

NEVER CAN SAY

Farewell down the phone
I need a separation doula
for your breezy parting words.

Weep through breakup movies,
hum sad songs asking why
lip sync cold car karaoke.

Construct forlorn mix tapes
feeling like I'm gonna die
write postcards never sent.

Ardent continents part
singing familiar wailing song
reverb blue guitar resounds.

You pulled the plug
curtained sunlit sky
I'm shivering in the bath.

You're streaking down the straight
I'm still lacing up my shoe
reflecting in your slipstream.

Suppression impulse stifles
last regrets squeezing by
your finger pressed against my lips.

Is lost love better left?
Know you've got to fly
I can't start to find an end.

Later on the street of dreams
pretty faces smile and pout
recalling memories deeply burned.

SEEKING SINGULAR

Nights in front of shining screens
seeking clandestine pairing
in similar singular situation
for sheet-stretching, quilt sharing.

Weavers spinning a world wide web
whisper ecstatic sighs of cognition
discovering resonating fibres
of transmissible textual recognition.

Where have you been all my life?
Loving the way we talk
mother tongue of intimacy
takes our senses for a walk.

Getting high on SMS projections
neurotransmitters surge with oxytocin
pursuing, submitting, having,
in an enchanted biologic ocean.

Emotions, feelings, 'chemistry',
seeking 'one and only'
that heals childhood wounds
rather than leaves you lonely.

In make-believe world
magic selves love each other
in-jokes now not quite so funny,
stifle laughter you want to smother.

Once adorable little quirks
become downright annoying
suddenly you're needing space
rather than lovey-dovey cloying.

Emotional gaffer tape won't save it
indifference equals disconnect,
down the track you'll feel better
dragging your self-respect.

Connections start breaking up
all the friends who gave you flak
suitors you couldn't hack
lovers who stabbed you in the back.

Unanswered calls trembling in your pocket
illuminating dark corners of your indignity complete
let your fingers do the talking,
block caller, highlight contact, press delete.

LOVERS

Having loved, fought,
withdrawn and wept,
they lie like wise bookends
symmetrically enclosing brawling camaraderie.

Exhausting exponential desire-aversion
reflections on existential unsatisfactoriness
provide momentary relief
from threshing emotions.

Finally collapsing post-precipice ascent
in mutual surrender
refreshing tidal waves
of tender mercies.

POETCCHIATOS

EQUALITY

Jack's as good
as his master,
more or less,
everything being equal
Jill fearfully
skirts night streets.

KING COAL

Stubbie holders of the realm
girt by girth's own goal
bursting motherland's apron strings
toasting old King Coal.

NEIGHBOURS

Ordinary decent bloke
mowed the lawns
kept to himself
went to work everyday
kids always clean,
shot the lot.

GRAVITY

You don't need
to be Newton
to know that
too much gravity
brings you down.

BROKEN

Can Wabi-sabi put
heartbroken Humpty together again?
Love Glue,
never travel without it.

HOMELESS

Love needs
a place to stay,
can we fix up
the spare room?

ALL I KNOW

Socrates knew
one thing, nothing.
Marx denied he
was a Marxist.

AFTER FUKUSHIMA

I am become Death
destroyer of worlds,
bitter lava drowns
Thousand Goddess bathhouse.

VOW

Downturned begging bowl
empty of bowlness
full of emptiness
all vows useless.

BLUE EXISTENCE

LOVE BOAT

In the name of love
drop the blame game, the lame game,
of I dump all over you
while wishing unconditional loving kindness
to me, me, I, I and everyone else,
except the ex-wife
or the current relational strife.

Be on Cloud Nine,
discovering life's gold mine,
ants foraging in a sweets larder
sharing amore with the Gods
Shiva and Parvati, Krishna and Radha,
or those other lovers on our planet
from Romeo and Juliet to Brad and Janet.

Don't listen to the cynics,
their mimics, moralisers and patronisers shouting
too old, too young, too heart, too head,
ending up instead irradiated
by endless cathode hours
on chip-encrusted TV spud lounges,
hearts hardened like centuries-old parmesan.

Stay true, let yourself go
in the retrovision
of silly love songs.
Love Is in the Air (breathe in)
Stop! In the Name of Love (pause, reflect)
Love Hurts (note pain)
All You Need Is Love (realise).

You can be the Loved One, star in the Love Story,
sail on the Love Boat, join the Love-In, contract the Love Bug
or stay in the Love Shack, have a love attack,
be love-sick or even a love junkie,
because for love or money like bees to honey
love makes the world go round but
comes, and goes, without a sound.

In the name of love
stay awake, remember the love you give
is equal to the love you take
just when love seems in vain
don't weep too long
get up off the floor,
love just came in the door.

LET GO

Nothing you crave
travels to the grave,
all that you desire
burns on your funeral pyre.

The fortune you've acquired
all the accolades desired,
merely kindling piling higher
to feed your final fire.

The endless stories told
ad nauseam narratives of old,
who writes the lyric, sings the song,
she was right, you were wrong.

But, of course,
the carousel spins off course,
you're glued to your saddles by centrifugal forces
mirror images waving from horses.

The words go round and round,
and up and down,
and round and round,
'til you're dizzy on the ground.

Trapped inside the cling wrap of life
Weltschmerz and Sturm und Drang are rife,
you blame your husband, or your wife,
for your collectively constructed strife.

Unpack, peel back, reveal
the transparency of the deal,
extract the sting, breathe in
and sing, L-E-T G-O.

L-E-T G-O, L-E-T G-O
watch everything just flow
everybody's seen the show
let go, let go, let go.

BOOZE NATION

Booze nation!
Our collective shadow since before Federation,
overlaying infantile grief of separation
from our land, ourselves,
what we did to the 'other',
the kids, the dog,
sister, brother, father, mother,
staggering in consensual seizure
under our national anaesthesia.

Fuelling murderous desires, igniting familial fires
'fuck you, fuck me, fuck everyone, fuck the lot of ya!'
Hiding shame, concealing blame, extracting the sting,
'it was the grog talking', 'I was blind at the time',
'pissed as a newt', 'can't remember a thing.'

Booze nation!
Creative stagnation, psychic disorientation, emotional
constipation, fluid inflation, eros deflation,
the national grog toll records
burned out remains of human conflagration,
puffed up pride, 'greatest country on earth', 'best beer',
all pissed down the drain,
I'd drink you under the table,
but I'm outta here.

The country unites over a glass or two
or three or four or maybe more
one for the road, have another one, get it in ya,
individuality's bedevilment, life's great leveller,
liquid penile shriveller.

Booze Nation!
We're legends, larrikins, and egalitarians,
the spew of being under the weather
holding us together
in a conspiracy of self-sedation.
Hey mate it's your shout!
Imagine this country
with enough energy to light up the wattle,
on the wagon, off the turps, at full throttle.

EVERYMAN BLUES

Everyone wants an Everyman
pre-and-post feminist astute
an Armani-clad troubadour
providing forbidden fruit
moved by a van man
wooed by a candyman
a cleverman that tricks it
a handyman to fix it.

Man of God, man of tomorrow
man of peace, man of sorrow
metrosexual man, new man branding
street fighting man, last man standing
a man to watch, fine man as such
sadder and wiser man, man who knew too much
man's inhumanity to man, make a man out of you
a man's gotta do what a man's gotta do.

Big man, small man
fat man, tall man
man up, man down
marked man, man clown
company man, hatchet man
yesterday's man, boogie man
man below, man above
man date, man love.

Man of the moment, man on the take
man in the middle, man on the make
man of the cloth, man on the street
Man in the Moon, man on the beat
man with a plan, man of the match
man of his word, a man to catch
man in a hurry, man of the house
not half the man, man or a mouse.

Best man, hanged man
rich man, poor man
straight man, thin man
nowhere man, tin man
journeyman, postman
freeman, Bergman
watchman, Third Man
Sandman, Birdman.

Many roles to choose
every one bound to lose
gonna ask the shaman
to make a hu-man out of me,
there's a man crying on the news
can't pay his dues
TV doctor says
he's got the Everyman Blues.

Man after my own heart
wrong man for right reasons
no man is an island
man for all seasons,
every inch a gentleman
man of wealth and taste,
behind every great man
another man gone to waste.

Manhole, mansplain
Mandrake, Man Ray
manhandle, manbag
Godman, man rag
Superman, Batman
Spiderman, Catman
policeman, Iceman
Dogman, Diceman.

Man with the golden arm
old man and the gun
man who sold the world
man on the run
true measure of a man
a man of worth
man who did no harm
man who fell to earth.

Mantrap, manless
mangrove, manliness
manhandle, manhood
man slut, man boob
my man, sly man
foot man, Pac-Man
blues man, funny man
news man, dunny man.

Man of few words
man on the land
man of letters
one man band,
busman's holiday
blindman's bluff
dead man walking
are you man enough?

So many roles to choose
every one bound to lose
gonna ask the shaman
to make a hu-man out of me,
there's a man crying on the news
can't pay his dues
TV doctor says
he's got the Everyman Blues.

Walk like a man
man on the shelf
fight like a man
every man for himself
one man's love
another man's meat
man of the year
man to beat.

Man in a hurry
man on the edge
holdup man
man on a ledge
man of desire
man on the door
man on fire
man o' war.

Man of steel
man in the tower
man on the loose
man of the hour,
man oh man
Everyman Jack
go-to man
Man in Black.

Man out of time
man runs his course
every man has his day
A Man Called Horse
walk like a man
man out for a jog
give a man a break
man bites dog.

First man, last man
real man, hollow man
hard man, bad man
wise man, madman
ladies' man, man's man
pants man, bag man
fireman, snowman
straw man, no man.

All these roles to choose
every one bound to lose
gonna ask the shaman
to make a hu-man out of me,
there's a man crying on the news
can't pay his dues
TV doctor says
he's got the Everyman Blues.

THE GREAT REVELATOR

Went to see the Devil
he asked what's up?
I'd seen a man about a dog
but he sold me a pup.

Judas betrayed Jesus for 30 silver pieces
everyone has their price,
before the rooster crowed
Peter denied him thrice.

Many men have fallen
others can't speak
some men are crawling
a few are too weak.

Station master takes my bags
sensing my unease,
says, 'Where you're going pal
you won't be needing these.'

Inside the darkened carriage
not a word is spoken,
splintered seats are empty
my ticket but a token.

Single car runaway
engine driver's stood down,
I'm riding the Great Revelator
all the way outta town.

Judah the lion lamb,
seven horns and seven eyes,
breaks Seven Seals under seven angels
trumpeting the skies.

Sword of Damocles
hangs over the final feast
diners choke on horsehair
studying the menu of the Beast.

Six six six signals
end-time of the system,
four horsemen riding past,
gone before you missed them.

Pale horse approaches
in bloody carnage to revel,
ridden by death,
followed by the Devil.

Humankind shall flare
in eternal fires,
fuelled by bone-dry tinder
burning our desires.

Hiding my religion
disguised as a clown
I'm riding the Great Revelator
all the way outta town.

Witness in the watchtower
resisting deep somnolence of death,
inhaling darkest night
transforms morning's breath.

Conclusion of all things
marks the ending of an age,
renew our precious earth
by turning the page.

Among disaster's apathy
conceit's piper plays the tune,
war, famine, plague
cast the planetary rune.

Ghosts wander aimlessly
through indifferent lands,
the healer walks among them
laying on of hands.

'Love your neighbor as yourself'
whispers the Holy One to the wise,
comfort those homeless among you
as angels in disguise.

Sliding through the stations
green fields turning brown,
I'm riding the Great Revelator
all the way outta town.

PANDEMIC BLUES

I come from another era
crossing borders with ease
I'm untouchable baby
do what I please.

From ancient Greece
to the Roman Empire
through the Middle Ages
I'll set your house on fire.

Forget all your theories
I'm here to testify
a force of nature
just want to multiply.

Don't care about culture wars
who's wrong and who's right
I'm gonna infect you
whether you're black or white.

I float in the air
sting in the breeze
a silent assassin
in a cough or a sneeze.

Stop killing the wild
clear felling the trees
I'm your worst nightmare
the Anthropocene Disease.

From Wuhan to Washington
Paris, London and Rome
I'm what you sowed
and honey I'm home.

Nothing to do
but pay your dues
my time has arrived
I'm the Pandemic Blues.

Pandemic Blues
Pandemic Blues
I'm a killer baby
and I'm coming for you.

Previous performances

'The Months' was performed by the author at the Darebin Music Feast in 2012 to music composed by Amadis Lacheta. 'As I Passes By', 'Fullness of Time', 'Memento Mori', 'Coming and Going' and a version of 'Last Night' were spoken by William Zappa in a 2015 ABC Classic FM recording of composer and viola player Romano Crivici's music 'Reflections on Life, Death and Transience'. Several live performances of this suite of music and text were also staged in Sydney and Europe.

Acknowledgements

Gratitude to my late mother Betty, father Colin and maternal grandmother Florence without whom I would not exist nor have survived that existence. Love to my comrades in arts, Geoff Young, Denni Scott Davis and Amadis Lacheta for their encouragement and thoughtful support. A huge thank you to my empathic editor Ross Gillett for his guidance and generosity. Deep appreciation for proofreading by Paul Majewski and Estella Vinecombe. Maximum respect to energetic and ever-responsive publisher Gordon Thompson for giving this collection a shelf life. A deep bow to all the poets from whose creativity and spirits I have drawn sustenance throughout my life.

About the author

Gerald Frape is a writer and social cause communication strategist. He has written for *Source*, *Broadside*, *Digger*, *Nation Review*, *National Times*, *Penthouse* and *Australian Yoga Life*. He was founding editor of *The Bush Telegraph* magazine, media director for the NSW 'Quit' anti-smoking campaign, and communications consultant to the National AIDS Advisory Committee. Gerald has also consulted to the WHO and a range of Australian government and NGO campaigns. He has lectured on social cause communication at universities in Sydney and Melbourne. His short plays have been performed in Sydney's Short and Sweet Festival and the Melbourne Fringe Festival. This is his first published collection of poems.

www.ingramcontent.com/pod-product-compliance
Lightning Source LLC
Chambersburg PA
CBHW032237080426
42735CB00008B/888